MADE TO TREMBLE

MADE TO TREMBLE

HOW ANXIETY BECAME THE BEST THING THAT EVER HAPPENED TO MY FAITH

BLAIR LINNE

B&H PUBLISHING®
BRENTWOOD, TENNESSEE

978-1-4300-9636-8

Published by B&H Publishing Group
Brentwood, Tennessee

Dewey Decimal Classification: 616.85
Subject Heading: PANIC DISORDERS / PEACE—
RELIGIOUS ASPECTS / GOD

Cover design and illustrations by David Wardle.
Author photo by Maria Orlova.

1 2 3 4 5 6 • 28 27 26 25

For the faith-filled tremblers, who
have been made to feel shame.

Acknowledgments

"Don't be anxious about writing a book about anxiety," were the words spoken by my husband that would later swirl around in my mind when I was feeling anxious about writing a book about anxiety. I signed the contract for this book and about a week later thought, "What am I doing writing a book on anxiety!?" Throughout this process, his words not only came to mind but made me chuckle. Shai, although your words were not prophetic, they kept me going. Also, thank you for the practical ways you stepped in to hold things down when I needed those evenings at the coffee shop or days away to write. I sincerely appreciate your comfort when I started this project and had to push the timeline back when I lost my mom to cancer. For months, I could not depend upon my mind to craft sentences, but I could depend upon your love. Thank you.

To Sage, Maya, and Ezra, I am honored to be your mom. It is one of my favorite joys. I think this was the first project where you realized I have a job. As you read the books your dad and I write, may you appropriately appraise the glorious Jewel of heaven so that through a holy valuation, grace will leave accounts once in the negative, with pockets and purses full. May God be your most treasured asset.

I am grateful for Connie Dever, who immediately reached out to me when I was still hazy about what those panic attacks meant. Thank you for the resources, calls, and the visit to Philly, even navigating an unfamiliar train system to care for me face-to-face. I will never forget your sacrificial love.

Thank you to Nancy Wolgemuth and Revive Our Hearts, who, when I had to pull out of a conference in 2017 due to crippling anxiety, recommended a counselor; and suggested rather than return the honorarium, they encouraged me to use it to pay for my first group of counseling sessions. Thank you for introducing me to Sheila Stately, who counseled me through my suffering and pointed me to hope, Scripture, and practical help.

Ms. Sheila, walking into your office was not always easy, but I was always better for it. I shared with you the ins and outs of my life but didn't have to explain culture because you understood. Thank you for living outward and comforting others with the comfort of Christ. In one of those sessions, you encouraged me to write about my experience. I am confident this book is partly the result of that nudge.

To Risen Christ Fellowship, thank you for walking with me during my years of anxiety and offering practical care by generously paying for counseling out of benevolence when we were living on a tight pastoral salary. Also, to the many sisters who created a schedule to care for practical needs when I could not care for my family, thank you. You came over and folded clothes, set up meal trains, and offered your presence even when you didn't understand what was happening with me. Thank you.

Bobbi Jo Yarborough, thank you for your generosity in reading over the book and making detailed comments that I know made this book so much better. Also, thank you to my friends (Sasha, Elisabeth, Trent, and Lisa), who contributed to the book by adding a piece of your story to point to God's grand story.

I am grateful to my agent, Austin Wilson at Wolgemuth and Wilson, for partnering to minister to the world with words. Thank you for the encouragement to step out in faith with this book.

I am also so grateful for my editor, Ashley Gorman, and the brilliant team B&H put behind this book. Thank you for being so patient as my grief changed our schedule and for the much-needed rewrites of drafts to get this book to where it is today. I appreciate that you invested in me as a person and a writer. This project grew me in a way, and that is only because of your careful handling of me during this process.

I want to acknowledge my mom, Jeri Wingo, who passed away on September 27, 2023. When I was nine years old, my mother would take me to a writing workshop at the World Stage in Leimert Park every Wednesday night. She knew I also loved to write. Despite my young age, she invested in me. I am grateful for that sacrifice, as writing is one of the primary gifts I use today. Thank you, Mother, for how you saw me and gave it your best.

And what more can I say? This book was a team effort. Many more friends have come alongside to offer help and kindnesses that were a means of grace to me, without which I am certain I would not be where I am and, as a result, this book would not be.

Yahweh, thank you. Whether I am anxious at this moment or not, your presence is always my peace.

Contents

Foreword

There is a New Testament verse that has become a friend to me. It is 2 Corinthians 4:7–10 (ESV).

> But we have this treasure in jars of clay, to show that the surpassing power belongs to God and not to us. We are afflicted in every way, but not crushed; perplexed, but not driven to despair; persecuted, but not forsaken; struck down, but not destroyed; always carrying in the body the death of Jesus, so that the life of Jesus may also be manifested in our bodies.

This passage is at once both deeply humbling and powerfully encouraging. The apostle Paul likens you and me to jars of clay. A jar of clay is not a picture of strength but of being fragile and weak. If you drop a jar of clay, it will shatter into pieces. With these words, our delusions of independent strength are shattered. Independently strong is not who we are because that is not what God created us to be. We are all weak; there's no denying it. We lay down empirical evidence of our weakness every day. So, it is vital for our spiritual and emotional health and for the sanity of our relationships that we make peace with our fragile clay-ness. This means in God's great, wise, and loving plan, weakness is not an obstruction in the way of the plan, but an intentional part of it. So, our big problem is not our weakness; no, it's our assessments of strength.

Weakness is meant to preach the gospel to us. It is meant to remind us that we are not okay left on our own. It is meant to preach the truth to us that we were made to be willingly and joyfully dependent on God, that is, to find our strength, security, and rest in him. Assessments of independent strength preach a false gospel of autonomy, that we can live well without God. So, weakness is not a curse; it's a portal, a doorway into the best, most wonderful life ever, the kind of life that is only found when you find your strength and rest in the One whose storehouse of strength is infinite. It is both scary and a blessing to become comfortable in admitting that we are all a collection of weaknesses held together by cords of divine grace.

What does this have to do with anxiety? Anxiety is God's exposé. It is one of the many ways He confronts us with the inescapable reality of our weakness. He uses anxiety to reveal our weakness, not as an action of mockery or condemnation, but as a response of redeeming love. In exposing our weakness, God is wrapping arms of divine love around us and drawing us near to find in Him what we cannot find in ourselves or in anything or anyone else.

Now, this is where the 2 Corinthians 4 passage gets exciting. It preaches something to us that we desperately need to hear and understand. Understanding what Paul says next will change your life, maybe even in ways you didn't think were possible. Paul wants you to know that God has given you something enormously better than a weakness-free or anxiety-free life. What He has given you is the gift of gifts. What is that amazing gift? God has given you Himself, and with Him comes everything that you need. This is the one life-transforming place where the Giver is the Gift. So, weakness is not your enemy. It is God's means of bringing you to accept who you are and to celebrate what you have been offered in Him. We are the cracked clay pots; He is the ultimate treasure. In the cracks of our weaknesses, fears, and anxieties, His divine power and glory shines through, reminding us and the watching world of what can only be found in Him.

Second Corinthians 4:7–10 is why I love *Made to Tremble,* this book you hold in your hands. It's like Blair Linne decided to use her anxiety to unpack the power and practicality of this passage. I love the street-level honesty, transparency, and practicality you find here. I love that this book doesn't treat anxious people as disembodied souls but recognizes our body-*and*-soul nature. Anxiety is a heart problem (inner man), anxiety is a body problem (outer man), and it must be dealt with on both fronts. In so doing, we honor God, who designed us as both physical and spiritual beings. Through Blair's story, we get to eavesdrop on a wonderful catalog of insights gained, practical strategies learned, and divine comforts received. Watch out—this book may change your life!

We all live in a world that is groaning, not functioning as God intended, waiting for redemption. Because this is what God has chosen to be our address between the "already" and the "not yet," suffering is a universal human experience. If you're not suffering now, you will some day, and if you're not suffering now, you're near someone who is. But here is the good news. Our suffering, weakness, and anxiety are not ultimate; God is, and because that is true, there is a day when we will be weak no more. He will finally free us of the burdens of our suffering, to live with Him in uninterrupted peace and righteousness forever and ever.

Right now, suffering still lives with us, so I recommend this book to you. It will fill you with practical wisdom, but best of all, it will build your confidence in the presence, promises, power, and grace of your Lord. I am so thankful for what you are about to read in Blair's words, and I'm sure you will be too.

—Paul David Tripp
pastor, award-winning author, and conference speaker

Introduction

Are the waves of anxiety crashing around you? Can you feel them rising, threatening your breath? Are you just trying to keep your head above them? If you've picked up this book, you have likely experienced—or are in the middle of experiencing—the daily struggle anxiety brings as it pulls you into its depths. For you, it may be an ominous surge, a torrent, threatening to inundate you. Or maybe it's more subtle, like standing at a shore, understanding that there are unknowns out there in the depths, wondering if you might be overtaken any moment. Or perhaps your experience is more like a mix of erratic waves, or like a sneaker wave, catching you unaware, lifting you off your feet at unpredictable times.

Regardless of exactly how you have been swept into anxiety's undertow, there is often no warning. No cautionary "danger: strong currents" sign to prepare you. As someone who was initially swept off my feet and overwhelmed, I stand in solidarity, dripping wet with you. I offer this book as a life ring.

As I consider all God has taught me, I can say something now that, when the waters engulfed me and I was at the bottom of the sea, I never thought possible, and that is this: I went from believing that anxiety was the worst thing that could happen to me to now knowing that anxiety became one of the best things that has ever happened to my faith.

You may wonder how I can say that. The reasons for this statement are manifold and what I will attempt to communicate in this book. Overall, I can make this statement because I have come to see that being a conqueror is not measured by never feeling anxious again. I realize this is not the prevailing litmus test for victory we are so often taught. We are told to measure our success or failure with any given struggle based on how well we keep it at bay. If we sense the struggle on a certain day, we have failed the test. If we don't sense it much at all, we have succeeded. This is not how the Bible handles our struggles, ailments, or weaknesses. To sense struggle is not victory or defeat in and of itself. To feel our weakness in the face of suffering is not failure. In fact, to feel the acuteness of our fragility and acknowledge the acuteness of God's divinity opens a portal to true success, which is a deep dependence on a never-anxious God.

I was surprised by this discovery because a lot of teaching on anxiety will tell you that to overcome it, the person you need to understand and depend on most is *you.* If you take these ten courageous steps and find strength within yourself by mustering up enough mental power, you will conquer the waves of anxiety like a pro-Olympic surfer and become the champion of your own story. But you will not find much of that in these pages since the first-place award is not up for grabs. It is awarded to the One who is over the winds and waves. Understanding yourself and developing insight is a good thing (we'll do some of that), and there are certain mental exercises that are helpful when it comes to combatting anxious thoughts (we'll do some of that too), but *depending* on yourself to fix something as big as anxiety? That is another thing entirely. That is why you'll find that my intent in this book is not to rile you up into a motivational moment. Instead, I ultimately desire to lift your eyes from all that swirls in your own head and up to the Prince of Peace, because He is the true hero of our story. One of the most courageous things you can do is ask Him for help.

Victory in anxiety, for me, has been found by experiencing this deep dependence on God. And that is something I can do on a particularly anxious day when I feel as though I'm drowning, or on the days when I'm at the edge of the shoreline. As it turns out, anxiety was not an obstacle that I needed to avoid; it was a portal to a person I needed to behold: Jesus Christ. And so, I learned that every trembling trial we face is another push toward Him. I now no longer ask myself, "Did I avoid the wave of anxiety today?" Instead, I ask myself, "When I feel the wave, big or little, who will I depend on?"

I can say that through the lessons learned in this book, my difficulties with anxiety have indeed lessened. But I cannot know if that will remain the case. The Bible promises that in this world, we will have trouble,[1] so I can be assured that there will always be an opportunity for anxiety. I may re-enter a stronger anxiety storm than I've faced thus far. Or, in spite of the world and by God's grace, I may continue to recover from anxiety, even experiencing a miraculous and total release from its grip. But here's something I know to be true either way. Even if I never again tremble in the ways I have, I never want God to take away what I have learned in my most anxious season thus far—the weakness that led me to dependence and reliance upon the Lord. The ability to rejoice in what God is doing despite how I feel. The opportunity to see the heavenly realities that go beyond earthly boundaries and burdens. The endurance to find hope when circumstances seem bleak and hopeless. God has graciously lifted my eyes upward to see that victory is in Jesus, even when my steps falter because my body feels broken. In the seasons when anxiety's waves have crashed onto my frame and I've trembled to my core, I have learned what it is to lay hold of the only anchor that can sustain us in the trying waters, and that is Christ. We all *know* we should lay hold of Him, of course. But I have actually done it, I've been forced to do it. Charles Spurgeon said, "They who dive in the sea of affliction bring up rare pearls."[2] In this sea, I've laid hold of him in the past few years in ways that I never knew were possible. And I can confidently say now that no matter the bait thrown out by the enemy, I wouldn't give up the pearls I received underwater, deep in my lament. Those lessons and pearls include spiritual things, of course. But they include other things too, for anxiety is not *only* a spiritual thing. It involves the whole person. And so, expect to see words from me that range as far and wide as the human experience does, which brings us to what to expect in this book.

I am not an expert in the field of mental health. Know that I am speaking, not as a trained counselor, but as someone who has experienced anxiety and trembling. While I have had experts read this book to verify its helpfulness, I'm not going to give you an anxiety manual. My goal as a sister in Christ is to put before you the lessons I learned

1. John 16:33
2. Charles H. Spurgeon, sermon "The Golden Key of Prayer" (March 12, 1865), *Metropolitan Tabernacle Pulpit Volume 11.*

and passages that have been most instructive to me as I persisted through the worst and best parts of learning to manage my anxiety and develop a different relationship to it.

As you read through these pages, you'll see that I start off by sharing my story of how I met anxiety. The truth is, my story is the story of the human race since we are all afraid in some way. I invite you to explore with me the origin story of humanity and the *why* behind this universal experience; we'll explore different kinds of fear. What is beautiful is how God engages us amid our anxiety; and it might be different than what you might typically think. Then, I write about the surprising fact that while we weren't made to be shaken, there are ways in which we *were* made to tremble. We'll explore what it looks like to let God rule over your life instead of anxiety. I write about how we are more than a soul (since God has created us as whole beings—body, soul, and spirit), and how that should all weigh in on how we think about our experience and the tools available to help us. I share tips I have learned along the way through counselors and friends who have also experienced anxiety. You'll also see a chapter about how we can be helpful when it's time to care for those we love who are anxious. I write about how God helps us in our experience with deep anxiety when we cling to Him. We can cast our cares upon Him and even "do it scared," with His help. I primarily share scriptural encouragements along with some physical helps to ease symptoms and manage stress.

Oh, and one thing to know about me: Since I'm a poet and spoken word artist, I write in poetry and prose. You will see a mix of poetic writings and poetry throughout the book. A final word that feels fitting for a book like this: If you are in urgent need of help in your anxiety journey, there are some numbers and websites, breathing techniques, promises, prayers, psalms, and a poem in the appendix section, along with a word to church leaders looking to help those in their care who struggle with anxiety.

Now that you know what to expect in this book, I'd love to close this introduction by praying over you and with you.

Oh Prince of Peace,

We tremble before You because You are the true and living God. I come on behalf of my friend who is afraid, anxious, trembling, because they are surrounded by cares. We are unsure of so much in our lives: our health, our home, our families, our churches, our country, our world. meet us in our individual storms. Calm our anxious bodies, hearts and racing thoughts. Help us to cast our cares onto You because You care for us.[3] *As our health, home, families, churches, country, and world feels out of control, remind us that You have full control. Every moment of our lives is known by You. In each fearful moment, You are right here with us. Thank You that You have not left us alone in our anxiety. You are the God who sees us . . . and comforts us in our sorrows.*[4] *Jesus, you are the God who incarnated to be familiar with our sorrows. In Your holy humanity, You modeled for us: "When [we are] filled with cares, your comfort brings [us] joy."*[5] *Help us to find You amid this suffering, that we might find Your joy. In the name of our Savior, Jesus, who suffered and trembled for us. Amen.*

---

3. 1 Peter 5:7
4. 2 Corinthians 1:3–4
5. Psalm 94:19

CHAPTER 1

Anxiety Knows My Name

My body shakes like hundred-year-old floorboards in a Southern revival. My clamoring heart takes center stage and preaches to me as the loudest voice in the room. *Lub-dub.* This pounding is given a mic, and everything and everyone else fades into a muffled blur. My wooden frame pulsates to the preaching. Heart stomping on the 1 and 3 and clapping on the 2 and 4 exposes me to nature's elements. Breath shallow. Mind foggy. Body frail. *Lub-dub.* My thundering heart tarries at the altar like a sinner waitin' on the Holy Ghost. Pearls of sweat gather on my skin like jewelry I never asked for. Anxiety wrestles me into submission. Waterlogs me until I release my deepest secrets. Awakens me with its thunderbolts. *Lub-dub.* This pouring rain never seems to close its faucet. It leaves me sopping, a crescendo of rage inside of me. *Lub-Dub.*

My thoughts swish, swirl, and crush like an ocean threatening to hold me under its rogue waves. Once the undertow takes hold of me, as though she wants to make me a tombstone out of her tears, I am left with questions ruminating like roaring rapids. *What are these erratic rivers that hold my body and mind captive? Why does my body tremble? Will things always be this way?* My head hurts. My heart is beating fast and hard like the strong hands of a church mother's distressed tambourine. She taps on-beat with the rain between stomps, reinforcing the grooved clothes that fit loose on sanctuary planks. *Lub-dub* grows louder and louder. I'm forced to surrender to its beating. Anxiety is my white noise. I wave my white flag. Float in this lake with hands outstretched.

I am like the disciples during the violent storm on the sea. Crying, "Lord, save us! We're going to die!" This trembling feels like I am approaching death. The waves swamp me. The rising suffering feels like Jesus is asleep. He is with me in the water, yet I ask, *Lord, are You asleep?* I can barely mouth, *Wake up, Lord, I am afraid.* Unlike the experience that the disciples had in Matthew 8:24–25, He does not rebuke these winds and waves immediately. I am with Jesus, and yet the waves rage on.

I can't take a deep breath. I barely swallow. I lie on my back, sinking in the high tide. I look past my ceiling to the sky. I know it's there, though obstructed by eggshell paint and an outdated ceiling fan clothed in the previous season's dust. My legs sink into my bed. They feel heavy. Chills radiate through my body. I pull up my sage-colored blanket. A minute passes, and now I feel like I am in a cup of green tea—hot, green, and earthy. I tell my husband to open the sliding door despite this East Coast autumn chill. I try to breathe, pray, and not worry. But I am afraid since my body is not working right. My once-clear vision is blurry. My mind spirals like a tornado. Anxiety has my thoughts running 1,000 miles per minute. My mind is not working like it once did when anxiety didn't know my name. Let me tell you about the moment we first became acquainted.

Anxiety Is a Beast

It's late and dark. The road is hugged by the beautiful autumn shades of an East Coast highway, but at this hour the trees resemble the shadows of a giant army. Only when high beams glimmer across the slick asphalt and the giants disappear do I catch the faint amber, ruby, and emerald jewels sparkling at the shoulder. It's just midnight, and my family and I are traveling to Grand Rapids from Philadelphia. My husband's eyes fade, so we decide to switch positions in our packed, rented minivan. He exits at the next rest stop and drives past the napping big rigs. He slides into the comfort of the reclined passenger seat. I slide into an upright position behind the wheel. Amid the thinned traffic there are flashing lights with signs warning me of deer season.

Stay alert. I watch the shadows to my right closely and drive in the left lane to avoid the wildlife and make good time. An hour or so into the drive, everyone else in the van is asleep. I'm in the fast lane, with no idea just how much my world is about to slow down.

Though I am vigilant to keep watch for any beasts lurking in the forest to my right, I am taken off guard from another surprising direction—my left. In an instant, in just the blink of an eye, something emerges—no, *darts out*—and faster than I can process, its huge frame jumps clear and high over the median wall that I previously assumed was protecting us by keeping danger out.

Here he was, a huge, heavy interruption crashing into my car and my life. A buck. The front of our rental van strikes the beast, causing the hood to fly up and slam onto the windshield. My husband jerks awake. I hear him scream and through the sliver of space where the hood doesn't cover my view, I see how the impact causes the muscular creature to spin and repel. It bounces off the bumper and to the far-right shoulder—effortless, like a child throwing a boomerang that would never return.

Little did I know, the impact of the beast *would* return, like a boomerang, fulfilling its purpose.

We eventually made it to Michigan and connected with family. The accident played in my mind like a silent film, the climactic scene in slow motion. After a short stay, we headed back to Philadelphia and for the next week or so I was fine. I drove down to DC by myself to attend a friend's engagement party. However later that day, ten minutes from home, all of a sudden, I felt like my throat was tied. I couldn't swallow. Despite it being November, I rolled down the window to take in the crisp air. I hoped the quick blast of chill would help me catch my breath. I thought maybe whatever was happening was the result of being tired after driving six hours. After a minute or so it was as if the Philly wind exhaled the air stored in its cheeks onto my face. My breathing returned to normal and I continued on my way home. I didn't think any more about whatever that hiccup was. Until it happened again.

A week later, while driving home from my small group by myself, I felt choked, unable to take in a deep breath or swallow. I had spent time with a few women who asked about the accident. I recalled all the crucial details: the deer, the crash, the smoking van, the shock. I didn't know this recollection would later be a trigger that set my body off. Like the previous time, I rolled down the window, but this time, the fresh air didn't help. After a minute of being unable to inhale, my insides went haywire, and my heartbeat increased. *Lub-dub. Lub-dub.* The pounding grew louder—louder—harder in my chest! Frantic, I called my husband. I told him something was wrong and that I needed a doctor immediately. He asked, "What is it? What's wrong?" Urgently I told him, "I don't know, but my heart is racing and I can't breathe. I think it's something serious. I've never felt this before." He told me he would be home to greet me and have a glass of water waiting for me. I quickly hung up the phone, thinking over his response. His suggested solution hit me. *Water?!* It was clear he didn't get the seriousness of this moment. This was unlike anything I'd felt, and water just would not do. I immediately dialed him back and firmly told him, "Water!? No. *I need a doctor!*"

I sped home, past stop signs, cruising through a red light or two. The way my heart was pounding, radiated through my entire body. *LUB-dub. Lub-DUB.* I felt slightly concussed. Then it hit me: *I must be having a heart attack.* I drove faster. *LUB-DUB.* My sweaty hands gripped the steering wheel. I tried to focus on the road, but everything was a blur. At home I parked the car. My husband was waiting to help me into the house. After guiding me into a chair I see the glass of water on the table. I insist we go to the ER. And we do.

The doctors didn't give me any clear answers. They just kind of looked at me. They ran a few tests, including an EKG. An hour or so later they returned to tell me everything was fine. *Fine!?* I think, *I certainly don't feel fine.* Although my body was calming down, I felt like I'd been close enough to smell death's breath. They gave me a pill and yes, some water. Cue my husband's displeased glance, which clearly communicates, "We have water at home, for free." It was still sitting on the dining table where he left it. No one told me what had just happened or what it all meant. Just that the tests were clear and I was fine. They sent us home with a discounted $3,500 bill. Overall, I felt grateful that my heart was calming down and I could breathe again. The invisible monster had left me. I felt somewhat safe, for the time.

What *Was* That?

I didn't know it then, but that was my first panic attack. If you've ever had one, you know it feels like you're dying or close to it. And since the doctors and nurses never told me what was going on, I would not have the language to allow me to identify this experience as a panic attack until a couple months later, after having several more.

If you've gone through it, you understand how complex this is. From the outside looking in, anxiety seems so simple—like a small puddle one can leap over if one has enough faith. Some pastors say that the anxious should be able to instantaneously snap out of all this fear—to hold faith like an illusionist holds *abracadabra* in their mouth—to make all the anxiety rabbits vanish underneath their spiritual top hat. Well . . . now I see anxiety is viewed as an illusion to others looking on, but to those of us who are familiar, it's an entirely different beast. We are not Houdini. We have faith, and anxiety is still there.

Anxiety Won't Give Up

My body wakes me up around the time of the accident every morning. I'm subconsciously thinking about deer and regularly jolted awake. While everyone else is asleep, my eyes are wide for hours between 1:00 a.m. and 4:00 a.m. because my body remembers my accident, even while I try not to. The terror that accompanies the jolts makes me fear sleep, even though I desperately need it. Insomnia, ruminating thoughts, and panic attacks are my new normal. A few times, I find myself questioning internally whether the accident actually happened or if I made it up. I mentally replay the deer hitting the van—*No, Blair. It's not a dream. It happened.*

The pace at which anxiety moves is hard to keep up with. It is contagious and now spreading into every corner and crevice of my life like a stream of water pushing through sand. It is consistently creating new pathways. I wake up anxious. What started as an encounter with a deer has now expanded to things that didn't bother me before. Driving. Speaking. Death. Church. Unfamiliar spaces. The possibility of having an anxiety attack at any time keeps me on edge. I never feel like myself. I am a changed person, weighed down by fears and angst.

I contact a few older women I used to attend church with and share what happened. I desperately need encouragement and I don't know anyone in my local church who has had a similar experience. Also, since we are a family in ministry, many members look to us to help counsel them rather than vice versa. I'm amazed as a few of these older women share their own struggles with phobias, obsessive-compulsive disorder (OCD), and panic attacks. Reading their emails is like having a warm cup of hot chocolate with a friend while snuggling in a blanket on a rainy day. Even though the rain is still pouring, their words are comforting, energizing, and protective. I don't feel judged at all. I no longer feel alone.

My former pastor's wife sends me a few books. One is an anxiety and phobia manual that explains how symptoms of anxiety are highly uncomfortable but not fatal. It says there is a difference between a heart attack and a panic attack and assures me that no one has ever died from a panic or anxiety attack. *Phew!* The fact that I'm not bound to die from anxiety is good news for me. That information helps me when the next panic attack strikes, and my heart begins stomping and beating like an overzealous drummer in a marching band.

Over time, I learn that panic attacks can occur when a person has been undergoing prolonged stress or has recently suffered a significant loss. It's the body's stress hormones triggering your body's "fight-or-flight" response. These hormones often elevate the heart rate and bring on symptoms like chest pain, shortness of breath, chills, dizziness, nausea, and/or cold sweats. While a heart attack may have similar symptoms, and the pain it causes may ebb and flow, typically, it doesn't subside. It often moves into your arm, neck, or jaw. Panic attack symptoms, however, eventually subside, and you come down from the adrenaline feeling a bit better afterward.[1]

A friend eventually asks if I've gotten my thyroid checked because hyperthyroidism can be masked as an anxiety disorder. The symptoms can show up as weight loss, palpitations, tremors, and anxiety. On the next trip to my primary doctor, I ask for a full thyroid blood panel to see if that's why my anxiety is dragging on long after the accident. He orders the labs, and the numbers are within range but low. Before I know it, an ultrasound is ordered, and a nodule is found on my thyroid. A biopsy is scheduled and the doctor confirms the results are clear. The nodule is benign. *Thank You, LORD!* However, he then goes on to emphasize the 5 percent chance that I might have thyroid cancer. He says he has experience, and he is confident that I have cancer just by looking at the exterior of my neck. I almost fainted in the office. I wasn't sure how I could be diagnosed with cancer when my biopsy was clear. I felt more anxious—*LUB DUB.* I called my husband in from the lobby. This was *not* what I expected, but could this be why my entire body was out of whack? My husband suggested we get a second opinion. The next doctor assured me of the opposite and scheduled ultrasounds to check on the nodule yearly to ensure it wasn't growing or showing any signs of concern. It wasn't. *Thank You, LORD.* But as you can imagine, this still did nothing for my day-to-day anxious symptoms. If anything, the newfound fear of cancer made them worse.

My primary physician (who I am on a first-name basis with now) never told me I had an anxiety disorder, but I remember a couple of years into these appointments, he handed me my visit summary that noted "Generalized Anxiety Disorder" in bold font.

Anxious People Have Cares

There can be a temptation to downplay life's stressors, burdens, and losses. But caring people have cares. Normal everyday people have

1. Edmund J. Bourne, *The Anxiety & Phobia Workbook*, 4th edition (Raincoast Books, 2005), 108–12.

cares. Anxious everyday people have cares. People have cares. Beyond the accident and subsequent anxiety episodes, there were several cares pressing in on our family. The big ones were financial, relational, ministerial, residential, and health cares. Maybe you can relate.

Financial cares

The whole reason my family had moved to Philadelphia was to plant a church. For my husband to take on a staff position in the heart of the inner city, his salary was cut by more than half. I remember being told that to maintain our health insurance through our sending church, we would have to pay $2,000 monthly for our family of five. This was impossible on our budget at the time, which is why we purchased insurance for our children and prayed for ourselves until we found a reasonable option. This is why I racked up such a high bill at the ER—I was initially uninsured. On top of this, the rental company sent us a bill for the rental damage that totaled $18,000. It took months for the insurance to cover the rental company's request. Those in-between months brought with them a cloud of fear and what-ifs that hovered over me: *What if the rental company doesn't foot this bill? What if we're stuck with an $18,000 van bill, along with a $3,500 medical bill, on top of all our other bills? How are we supposed to pull all this off on a modest pastor's salary?* Dealing with physical ailments from an accident brought financial cares because every appointment cost us.

Relational cares

This was my first time meeting new friends and church members in this new city. We had three children aged three and under. Our youngest was four weeks old when we moved. This new church we were so excited to start serving did not have childcare. I spent most Sundays sleep deprived, rocking children in the hallway, or listening to the sermon from a speaker in another room while I also wrangled our other small children. Since my husband was often preaching, he couldn't help. For several months, I took communion in that room, often in tears. The tears were not only a result of reflecting on the impact of Christ's death and resurrection. That was part of it, but many times I also cried about this death to the self I was presently living out. Death to my relational expectations. Death to feeling known. Death to sharing communion with the body. I felt alone and lonely. I didn't want to be by myself. And don't miss this: We took communion every Sunday. Being in that room reminded me *every seven days* that I was separated from others each week during that season. A worthy cause, to care for my beautiful little children, be mindful of the other attendees, and yet still, the death of my will and preference. So, I cried for the moments when Christ felt like my only community.

Ministry cares

My husband was one of the founding pastors of the church plant—meaning, when something needed handling, he was at the top of the list for the phone calls and texts and emails. It didn't take long to realize that pastoring in this context was not a traditional nine-to-five. It was hard to manage time. Now, my husband had been a pastor before but had never planted a church. Planting a church can be a lot more demanding. While ministry came with its joys, it also seemed there was always someone or something to be concerned about. I watched my husband bear the burden as he cared for suffering sheep. Because of the confidential nature of his ministry, he couldn't share those burdens with me, which meant that I couldn't help lighten the load for him. Though I couldn't know what was specifically in his heart and mind, I still cared about the burdens he couldn't disclose, and they weighed heavy on me just as they did him.

Household or residential cares

The first week of moving into our home, we were introduced to what would be years of house burdens. We turned on an upstairs shower, and water ran from that bathroom through the downstairs ceiling and found an exit through a recessed light in the living room. Thankfully, we hadn't yet purchased our couch because it would've become a sponge. We grabbed towels and a trash can to catch the ten-foot waterfall. Our house flooded a few more times within the first few months of being there.

When I first described our fateful road trip to Michigan, what I didn't mention is this: While we were preparing to depart for our trip, our basement was filled with three to four inches of water (due to old pipes backing up). We waited for our landlord to hire a water-damage professional to come extract the water, clean up the debris, and blow it all dry, but she never did. Despite our lease saying that flooding must be cleaned within forty-eight hours, our landlord dragged her feet like a child asked to leave Chuck E. Cheese. The water had been sitting for three days when we left. As a homemaker and homeschooling mom at the time, this triggered concerns about mold since we spent so much time at home. I wanted to break the lease or hold the owner accountable. It was difficult not to fear. *We had a beautiful, spacious house, but was it secretly filled with mold? Were we inhaling poison—and would we continue to for the foreseeable future?*

Health cares

As I said, I had just had a baby months before the accident. Recently, a friend of mine texted me, "Do you think you had perinatal anxiety back then?" I responded, "You know, I may have. There was so much going on with all of the cares and the accident that we never even thought to consider the fact that my hormones had not yet regulated from childbirth." We were told to look for signs of depression after birth. We were not looking for postpartum anxiety.

Maybe you can relate to these kinds of cares. Perhaps yours aren't the exact same circumstances as mine, but I imagine that if you're picking up a book like this, you've got some cares of your own. Money. Ministry. Relationships. Faith. Work. House stuff. Health. The cares can pile up on top of us, and we wonder if God made a wrong turn and got distracted on His way to providing for us.

He didn't.

I don't say that haphazardly. I've had to learn this over time. But I'm getting ahead of myself.

Anxiety Tsunami

This—all these swirling and unrelenting cares and concerns—is the context in which the car accident happened. Isn't that how it always happens? An endless number of hits only to be topped off by a final blow? Turns out, this is how tsunamis work. Tsunamis are not just one wave. They are a series of several. When I look back on that season of my life, I see it so much more clearly now: I was being hit from different angles. In survival mode. When at what felt like my worst, I was on bed rest, unable to do much of anything for weeks. I was trying to honor God. Make it through the day. Stay sane. Encourage my husband, children, and the church. I was trying not to be overtaken by all these waves. Said another way, the car accident was like the first domino falling in a line of troubles. One bumping the other, bumping the other until I was surrounded by an army of collapsed white tiles with black dots aimed at me. When the accident happened, all those black dots released their missiles, and I was left with trauma. All the cares I just mentioned, from the move to the accident, occurred within four months.

This was the context in which I was being told by a doctor (and myself, sometimes) that everything was fine. Yet, I was drowning in cares, thank you very much! I didn't feel fine. After that first panic attack, each time I got behind the wheel, I got strikingly nervous. The physical association of the car and driving told my body something that my conscious mind wasn't ready to acknowledge. My body was yelling, "Danger!" Because of this, every time I stepped into my car and started the engine, I was flooded with anxiety symptoms. I felt hot and needed to take off my jacket, even in the dead of a Philly winter. Things seemed okay the first five to ten minutes, but I felt faint driving beyond that. My mind was heavy and hazy as if I could doze off to sleep, and I had to push through the loud voice telling me to forget driving altogether. When it came to driving, I somehow knew if I refused to muster the will to keep making small attempts, it would make things worse because, mentally, I might completely lose confidence in my ability to drive. So I kept driving. Even though I could only drive in short stints, I drove. For months all I could do was make it to the grocery store five minutes away. I attempted to slowly increase my time behind the wheel every few months. Many days, I felt stagnant because my mind dreaded being forced to repeat the whole ordeal. *What if I hit another deer?* The onset of what-ifs pummeled me as though I were the deer that met my bumper that night. Over time, I got overwhelmed in the same flood of anxiety the psalmist experienced in Psalm 94:19 (ESV): *The cares of my heart are many.* And they weren't letting up.

So, there it is. The various ways and seasons anxiety learned my name. Some of my backstory. Read on and you'll see there is more that led me to this point, but I wasn't yet ready to realize all of that.

I imagine you have some sort of backstory with anxiety too, and I genuinely wish I could hear it. We could sit down together over a cup of hot tea and chat. So often, swapping stories helps a person feel less alone. I recommend you grabbing a journal and writing down your story. Yours may be far more intense than mine, or far less intense. But in the end, the intensity doesn't matter much, since anxiety feels like anxiety no matter who you are or what your origin story is. This means the lessons learned along the way can help us all in one way or another. Before we jump into some practical helps, let's turn to humanity's origin story and see how it connects to fear and anxiety.

CHAPTER 2

To Hide or Not to Hide, That Is the Question

Have you ever been out in public, and you just want to hide? Maybe you see someone you know but you are not in the mood to talk, so you linger a bit to avoid them? We recently joined a church with more than 450 members. Some Sundays, I feel overwhelmed at the thought of meeting another person or remembering another name. I have had several Sundays where, right at the benediction, I am slipping out the door. Don't get me wrong, I love people, but I also really enjoy being by myself sometimes. In those moments, I'm usually feeling much more introverted and anti-social, so I break for the door. I've also had my share of ducking down in a bookstore, sliding down another Target aisle, or lingering in the car a bit longer not to break up alone time. Now that I'm calling it out, I'm feeling vulnerable, but my name is Blair, and I have a confession to make: Sometimes I hide from people.

As it turns out, humans have been responding to fear this way since the beginning of time. Even if you know the gist, let's explore the ancient story of Eden, because in it lies the real reason anxiety exists in the first place. Before there was any fear, Scripture begins with these comforting words, "In the beginning God."[1] God. Elohim. The self-existent One. He is never afraid. He exists in the absence of anxiety. Peace is who He is and is shown in all He does. He takes chaos and ushers in order. He is always calm, never trembling or fidgeting.

1. Genesis 1:1

For whom would the Most High God tremble before, being that He is the greatest of all beings? Since He is all-powerful, no lesser being He created could stir any terror in Him. His steady, calming presence was in the beginning, is here now, and will always be. This is a great comfort to me, and hopefully an encouragement to you.

God possesses constant confidence, strength, and steadiness. He moves and gives out of His limitless pool of tranquil abundance. This is why creation was good. It was good because it reflected God's greatness and goodness. Creation's origin story is the effect of the artistic imagination of an All-Wise, All-Powerful Cause. It was good because creation is the outward expression of His creative order, holy character, and glorious rule. It was good because God was the center and orchestrator of it all.

Our Good Gardener

Creation was good because it was satisfied by a benevolent Gardener with generous provision. Humanity's home was a canvas for well-being. A well-thought-out garden with a myriad of luscious green hues. Plush and vibrant beyond what any eye could behold. A multicolored vegan feast surrounded Adam. Various trees created an abundance of food—not just for survival, but for enjoyment too—to satiate pre-Fall taste buds. Every direction displayed a lush landscape, supporting a variety of animals submitted to Adam, none of which had prey. Imagine: only harmonious chirps, howls, and songs. No murderous squeals. No fearful cries.

Eden was easy on the senses. The vibrant flowers beheld by eyes that knew nothing but overwhelming delight. The textures of plants touched by fingers that had never been caught red-handed. Still rivers moved slowly to water the peace-filled garden, heard by ears that had never yet listened to a lie. No late-night jitters or jolts since evening was as inviting as the day.

God's goodness meant there was harmony in creation. A God-established virtue where unity was the standard. Each element of nature God created was not competing with the others. They were all singing in tune, declaring the goodness of God. Seed-bearing plants, fruit trees according to their kind, lights to help with seasons and establish days and years, rivers to water the garden, animals to help create balance and beauty in the ecosystem, and mankind, charged to benevolently govern it all. God saw that His plan was good.[2]

> Then God said, "Let us make man in our image, according to our likeness. They will rule the fish of the sea, the birds of the sky, the livestock, the whole earth, and the creatures that crawl on the earth."[3]

Imago Dei is Latin for the image of God. It speaks to the immaterial part of our humanity and distinguishes us from the animals God created, allowing us access to commune with God in a harmonious relationship. In Eden, the primary relationship was with God.[4] But that did not mean God wanted Adam, His first human creation, to be alone. So, He created a wife for him.[5] Once the entire earth was created, along with man and woman, God took in all of His handiwork, and the Bible tells us this is how He viewed it: "God saw all that he had made, and it was very good indeed."[6]

Adam agreed with God's assessment, especially when it comes to the addition of woman. When Adam laid eyes on his wife, he was captivated, and the narrative tells us he showed himself to be an artist. A creator, like his God. A poet. Singing:

> This one, at last, is bone of my bone
> and flesh of my flesh;
> this one will be called "woman,"
> for she was taken from man.[7]

Adam and Eve lived in communion and conversation with God. There was joy. Abundant delight. The God who made them was in

2. Genesis 1:4, 10, 12, 18, 21, 25
3. Genesis 1:26
4. Genesis 3:8
5. Genesis 2:18
6. Genesis 1:31
7. Genesis 2:23

a relationship with them. There was no hindrance from God's good gifts because all their needs were met. It was a perfectly non-anxious world. God had plans for the future of the world, and the way He accomplished that future was by giving Adam and Eve a task, often called the cultural mandate.

> God blessed them, and God said to them, "Be fruitful, multiply, fill the earth, and subdue it. Rule the fish of the sea, the birds of the sky, and every creature that crawls on the earth." God also said, "Look, I have given you every seed-bearing plant on the surface of the entire earth and every tree whose fruit contains seed. This will be food for you, for all the wildlife of the earth, for every bird of the sky, and for every creature that crawls on the earth—everything having the breath of life in it—I have given every green plant for food." And it was so.[8]

Along with this mandate, God also gave them a command.

> And the LORD God commanded the man, "You are free to eat from any tree of the garden, but you must *not eat from the tree of the knowledge of good and evil*, for on the day you eat from it, you will certainly die."[9]

All in all, Eden was a world of endless blessings that came with one boundary. A world of yes, with one no—a no that, if obeyed, would protect Adam and Eve from harm, keep them immortal, preserve the perfect harmony of the cosmos, and maintain their unbroken and unfiltered relationship with God.

What love, truth, beauty, honor, provision, and freedom. Nakedness and exposure all around. But with no shame or fear or anxiety attached to it. Shame did not exist in Eden. Fear was unknown. There was no reason to ruminate on anxious what-ifs because everything was good.

---

8. Genesis 1:28–30
9. Genesis 2:16–17, emphasis added

There was no reason to cover up because even in utter exposure, there was nothing to hide. Until . . .

Choosing the Tree That Brings Death and Hiding from God

> The Tempter borrowed serpents' skin.
> To mask intent and mislead kin.
> Usurp Creator's words, though good.
> Now, fear exists where God once stood.

We know how the story goes. An enemy slithers into Eden. Who is he? "The ancient serpent, who is called the devil and Satan, the one who deceives the whole world."[10] From cover to cover, the Bible presents Satan as a deceiver, and when we read Genesis, we get a front-row seat to the first time he deceives humans. Here's how it unfolds:

> Now the serpent was the most cunning of all the wild animals that the LORD God had made. He said to the woman, "Did God really say, 'You can't eat from any tree in the garden'?" The woman said to the serpent, "We may eat the fruit from the trees in the garden. But about the fruit of the tree in the middle of the garden, God said, 'You must not eat it or touch it, or you will die.'"
>
> "No! You will certainly not die," the serpent said to the woman. "In fact, God knows that when you eat it your eyes will be opened and you will be like God, knowing good and evil." The woman saw that the tree was good for food and delightful to look at, and that it was desirable for obtaining wisdom. So she took some of its fruit and ate it; she also gave some to her husband, who was with her, and he ate it.[11]

---

10. Revelation 12:9
11. Genesis 3:1–6

The serpent twisted God's words, casting doubt on His character ("Did God *really* say that?"). Next, he outright lied about the consequences of crossing God's boundary ("No! you will not certainly die"), and then he held out the temptation of being their own god. Humanity took the bait. They ate, not from the Tree of Life, but from the Tree Forbidden. The father and mother of humankind disobeyed God's command, and just like that, their harmonious world was fractured in every direction imaginable. It was not until that foolish act of desiring and partaking of that banned branch that everything in our world drastically changed. It was this historical moment that stained every part of creation. Startled. Blemished. Broken. Like an orchestra creating a screeching halt on *Peer Gynt*'s "Morning Mood."[12] Now, good and evil abided not only in the garden, but in a war in the belly of mankind. "Their god is their stomach; their glory is in their shame, and they are focused on earthly things."[13] Death became a part of the human experience. Cue Mozart's "Lacrimosa."[14] In the blink of an eye—or rather a bite—the fall of man hit the world like a meteor, and now both mankind and creation suffer because of this descent from their glorious state.

What's the first effect of this great fall? What's the effect that multiplies into all others?

> Then the eyes of both of them were opened, and ***they knew they were naked;*** so they sewed fig leaves together and made coverings for themselves. Then the man and his wife heard the sound of the LORD God walking in the garden at the time of the evening breeze, and ***they hid from the LORD God*** among the trees of the garden. So the LORD God called out to

12. "Morning Mood" is part of Edvard Grieg's *Peer Gynt*, Op. 23, written in 1875 as incidental music to Henrik Ibsen's play of the same name, and was also included as the first of four movements in *Peer Gynt Suite* No. 1, Op. 46.
13. Philippians 3:19
14. *The Requiem in D Minor*, K. 626, is a requiem mass by Wolfgang Amadeus Mozart. Mozart composed part of the *Requiem* in Vienna in late 1791, but it was unfinished at his death on December 5 the same year.

> the man and said to him, "Where are you?" And he said, "I heard you in the garden, and ***I was afraid*** because I was naked, ***so I hid***."[15]

Do you see it? The moment sin was chosen, Adam and Eve became keenly aware of their fallen exposure before a holy God, along with the reality of death. As a result, for the first time in human history, fear was exalted in man's heart. This is the first time we hear of fear mentioned in Scripture. They've never been scared of God—never had a reason to be. And yet here they stood, in the home that God had made for them, afraid. At the moment of this conversion—from good to bad—this novel emotion eclipsed all of the goodness they enjoyed, and they were filled with fear. Anxieties multiplied. What-ifs consumed. The lush hues made room for dull, dim shades of doubt. Harmony between heaven and earth faded into a cacophony of chaos. And in this jarring discord, they heard the faint sound of God approaching, and they suddenly had a strange new impulse to hide.

Ever since that grave day in Genesis 3, this has been humanity's problem with God: feeling exposed to sin and death, which gives rise to fear and anxiety, which leads to hiding. We say along with Adam "I was afraid" of facing You and Your perception of me, God, "so I hid." We too run for cover because we're scared. Just like Adam and Eve, we hide. We slip out of church quickly because we are nervous about what we fear may be an awkward, or even condemning, interaction. And we're not alone. All of humanity and all of creation have groaned, hid, and been afraid since that day in the garden.

Hiding Behind an Improper Covering

Along with feeling exposed, and choosing to hide from God, there are two more things Adam and Eve did in response to their great fall: cover their nakedness with fig leaves and cover their sin through blame-shifting.

---

15. Genesis 3:7–10, emphasis added

> Then the eyes of both of them were opened, and they knew they were naked; ***so they sewed fig leaves together and made coverings for themselves.***[16]

Why did they sew leaves together? Why not just dart in the bushes and hide? Because feeling fearful and exposed not only makes you want to hide, but it also makes you want to cover up. We innately know this as humans. When someone does something terrible and tries to ensure no one will find out, we call their strategies a "cover-up" or "covering their tracks." There's a reason for that. When you know you're in the wrong, you try to conceal it. Adam and Eve were naked and unashamed prior to the Fall; but after, their disobedience made them want to cover up. And they did just that by:

Crafting clothes.

Tenebrous tailors

Stitching stalks and petals,

To pretend.

To patch and cloak.

Covering the glory lost

Masking the shame of newfound nakedness

For Adam and Eve, their nakedness was now synonymous with their sin. Their hiding was the result of a shift in allegiance. They thought the best solution was to fix it themselves. Not to move toward God, but to run away from Him.

The second way Adam tried to cover up his sin was by blaming his wife:

> Then he asked, ". . . Did you eat from the tree that I commanded you not to eat from?"

16. Genesis 3:7, emphasis added

> "The man replied. "The woman you gave to be with me—she gave me some fruit from the tree, and I ate."[17]

In the face of their sin-soaked conscience, they hid behind fig leaves and excuses. They ran away from the only one who could do something about their shame and clean up the mess they made. As God's original children, they could have had the attitude of the psalmist, who would later sing, "When my anxious thoughts multiply within me, Your comfort delights my soul."[18] But they did not run to God's comfort when their anxieties multiplied. If they only knew that hiding is the antithesis of how a child of an all-powerful, all-knowing, all-charitable Father should respond.

This feeling of exposure, this instinct to hide, this strategy of covering ourselves by way of fig leaves or blame-shifting—this is our inheritance from Adam. "Just as sin entered the world through one man, and death through sin, in this way death spread to all people, because all sinned."[19] As humanity's representative, the sin Adam committed expanded to the entire race, and we are all the recipients of that inheritance. We also individually choose to sin, showing that we are not merely a victim of our ancestors' sin, but we are active participants. There are so many ways that we try to hide the stain of living in a world shattered by that sinful ancient bite. When we are guilt-ridden and shame-filled, we hide. We hide in plain sight to take our minds off of what we fear: death.

We might think hiding behind fig leaves is a foolish thing to do when one is afraid of death but in truth, we all do the same thing, just in different ways. Everyone will face death. Often, it's not only that we will die but when and *how* we might die that can frighten us. When I received that janky cancer diagnosis, I never shared it with anyone but I remember thinking: *Well, maybe God is not calling me to help serve the church anymore.* I remember being concerned about not seeing my

---

17. Genesis 3:11–12
18. Psalm 94:19 NASB
19. Romans 5:12

children grow up, and I had fears about how my family would make out without me. What I was fearing was the unknown. We know ten out of ten people will die, but we don't want it to be a painful, slow death. So we hide. We hide behind our carefully crafted images, our social media feeds, our youthful products, sin, and excuses, or we throw ourselves into work and ministry, assuming that if we patch enough of these things together, we will avoid what is inevitable—judgment. As though what we hide behind will conceal what God already knows. The problem with fig leaves, real or metaphorical, is that they do not make for a proper covering for the aftereffects that come with something as damaging as sin.

The Whole Creation Groans

Adam and Eve's fall from grace not only brought sin into the picture, but at the heart of the rebellion was the introduction of suffering being a legitimate part of our human experience. We all feel the weight of suffering. The seashore is shrieking. This is not at all how things were when God first made the world and called it good, nor is this the way the world will be in the end, but this is the way things are now.

The reason we grapple with suffering and question "why" is because, deep within our gut, we know we are experiencing an unnatural phenomenon. Suffering is a part of the death that came because of Adam's sin. Just as humanity's representative (Adam) fell under a curse of decay (meaning, though he was once immortal, now he is able to die), all things under his care also fell under a curse of decay (that which God declared good is now liable to suffering).[20] Or, as God says to Adam, "The ground is cursed because of you."[21] Although the land is under a curse, it doesn't stay silent. Creation laments along with us—*groans*, in fact. "For we know that the whole creation has been groaning together with labor pains until now. Not only that, but we

20. Romans 8:20–21
21. Genesis 3:17

ourselves who have the Spirit as the firstfruits—we also groan within ourselves, eagerly waiting for adoption, the redemption of our bodies."[22]

It's not just humans who wail under the curse;[23] *all of creation* has been groaning in lament and will continue to groan as it "waits with eager longing" for Jesus to return and redeem all things[24]—whether visible or invisible—under His divine authority.[25] Until we are resurrected, glorified, and fully adopted, rescued from this fallen family, and brought into our new earth with our forever family, groaning is our collective language.

Until then, we know it in our bones: Things are not right. We all feel this deeply within us and observe it in our world. We can sense the curse of decay that the world is trembling under. We are hit with an abundance of sorrow at the spiritual, physical, mental, and social suffering in our world. From those separated from God, to natural disasters, injustices, emotional suffering, mental ails, chronic pain, wars, persecution, and collective suffering that people groups have faced or may face. Suffering and the anxieties that come with it are sometimes found in what would seem to be the most unlikely places—we find it in our churches and even our homes, just like how we found it in a plush garden. Unfortunately, suffering in all its variety is extensive and permeates everything everywhere. We groan at the fact that all of this is what is normative now.

How Does This Relate to Anxiety?

As we ponder the beauties and horrors of humanity's beginnings in Genesis 3, we realize that the birth of sin, suffering, and death brought with it fear. Not just fear of cancer, but fear of taking tests, imposter syndrome, or being afraid of not having money to feed a family. Anxiety is the response to feeling utterly exposed in front of God and others so we feel that we must push down core emotions for fear of

22. Romans 8:22–23
23. 2 Corinthians 5:2–4
24. Romans 8:19 (ESV)
25. Acts 3:20–21; Colossians 1:19–20

judgment. Anxiety is a natural reply to the reality of death. It is exactly what happens in our bodies when we sense some sort of threat—real or perceived. Anxiety is the knee-jerk reaction when we know we're in a mess, but we don't know how this deep, dark part of the story could ever be made right or reversed. We may end up anxious about a great many things in life—like car accidents and deer, for example—but all of them boil down to some version of these root issues. It's helpful to know their origins, the ways our fore-parents Adam and Eve hid them from God instead of taking them to Him. It's even more helpful—freeing—to know how God reverses these deep human problems and makes them right (we'll explore that in chapter 5).

The Temptation to Not Only Hide, But Isolate

When I think about running away and hiding from God, along with anxiety, I think of that famous scene in the movie *The Lion King*. It unfolds much like Genesis's account of the Fall. You likely know the story.

King Mufasa is a wise and generous ruler and father. He rules over the pride lands and shepherds his family with the values of kindness, benevolence, and harmony. King Mufasa tells his child, Simba, that he is preparing Simba to rule the pride lands, and he spends much time developing and shaping Simba so that the little cub learns to lead the appointed territory under his care according to the pattern of his father's own good rulership.

But a villain steps into the story and changes everything about this harmonious picture. Scar—the evil lion in the movie who is motivated by bitter jealousy toward King Mufasa—deceives the King's child, Simba. Though Simba has been told various truths by his father, he ends up forgetting the truths he knows and falling for the trickery of Uncle Scar. The fallout is terrible; his father, the great representative of all the pride lands, falls from the heights down into an irreversible demise. Just like that, Simba's father is forever ripped from him, along with his relationship with his family. And it's not long before the pride lands themselves fall under the sway of Scar, the evil one. The little cub is visibly anxious—eyes wide, darting, fearful, trembling, not knowing what to do.

The scheming voice of the evil Scar not only led Simba into this mess, but he's waiting on the other side of it, telling Simba how to respond to it: "No one ever means for these things to happen. But the King *is* dead. And if it weren't for *you*, he'd still be alive. Oh, what will your mother think?" he taunts Simba.

Exposure. Guilt. Accusation. What-ifs. And all the anxiety that comes with these things flood the little cub until tears overflow in his eyes. It is here that the most important moment happens: We learn what Simba does with his anxiety. "What am I gonna do?" asks Simba, terrified. "Run away, Simba," Scar hisses. "Run. Run away, and never return." Simba runs. For the second time, he trusts the voice of evil, darts toward the wilderness, and hides.

We can naturally see the parallels here to the Genesis story. But the worst part is that Simba does all of this in isolation. The next we see of him, he's languishing in the fetal position under the hot sun, with no one around to help him. Even when the jolly Timon and Pumba find him and probe at his story, he keeps all his groaning stuffed inside. Ashamed, he never willingly tells anyone who could help him. He stays in hiding, and no one knows but him.

The temptation when dealing with anxiety is not just to run away and hide, but to keep it to ourselves. Deep down, we often *do* want to go to God. We know that going to God helps us because He is our only resource to overcome this world. We know there is great comfort when we choose to be open about our afflictions, and we know being able to go to God when anxious is a beautiful privilege. But like Simba, against all the good truths we've been taught, we succumb to believing the opposite. We tell ourselves that our anxieties are just too strong for God to stomach. We think the intensity of our anxiety and suffering has caused us to make a mess of so much, including our relationship with our Father. We think we've worn Him out already, or that He'd be disappointed in us if we dared approach Him with just how out of control we are mentally and physically. Or we don't believe that God can handle our anxiety. So, in our wide-eyed and trembling anxiety, we listen to the hiss of the enemy and we run—from the One who could help us in the midst of it. As anxiety spears are projected, we dart away from our very Shield, meant to cover us.

But God does not want this. God pursues Adam and Eve, not only after the world's most colossal mistake (the sin of rebellion)—but also after the world's worst *anxious reaction* to that mistake (fear, hiding, covering up). God does not wait for them to figure out that their anxious response was misguided. He knows they have concealed their deepest issues and anxieties with improper coverings, and He moves toward them to cover them both up with something better.[26] He handles the problem with both parties present, allowing their healing to be experienced with Him instead of in isolation.

God knows their anxious responses to sin and suffering are going to fail them, and instead of abandoning them, He draws near to help them. He beckons them out of the shadows. He does the same with believers today. When we groan, He groans. When we hide, He seeks. He does more than that; He makes it so that there's no longer a reason to hide even if we do feel afraid. We'll explore *how* He does this in chapter 5, but for now, it is enough to say—and it is comforting to be reminded—that our God is a reconciling Father and He seeks to bring us back under His protection.

26. Genesis 3:21

CHAPTER 3

We Are All Afraid

Have you ever been swimming in the ocean and been caught up by a wave and it flips you upside down? For a moment you wonder if you will gain your bearings or not. That's what anxiety can feel like. Being flipped in undesirable seas. The mind swirls slowly and then picks up speed. Before you know it, the waters have risen above what you had as your boundary. The waves crash and break over you before you can have a clear thought. Here comes another wave. We often feel as though we are the only one spinning upside down. Caught by the wave. Drifting further from shore. Everyone else appears to be calmly floating and poised. Their life seems to be in control.

Friend, can I let you in on a secret? Lean in. Come close. Closer. It's pretty hush-hush, but as perfect as everyone around you may look . . . the reality is this: *We are all afraid.* All of us. It doesn't take each of us having an encounter with an actual serpent or a deer. Life knows how to buck and confront us with our own curated "deers," dear. No matter how strong we believe our faith to be. Not one of us living this side of Eden is exempt from feeling afraid. Deep within, we know this despite the difficulties we sometimes have admitting it to ourselves and others. Somewhere along the way we have all been taught that if we are afraid then we are in unbelief. But there is more than one way to be afraid.

Think about how we all reacted during the COVID-19 pandemic. Even if we were amongst those able to move past it relatively quickly, initially, we were all experiencing that basic human emotion: fear. As we wrestled with what an infectious disease might mean, we didn't know the specifics of how it was transferred, and it felt larger than us.

As a result, we felt fear within and observed this human emotion in others. Fear made us hoard tissue, stay in the house, wipe down our mail, move toward or away from a particular city, create community pods, and disinfect groceries. A friend recently confessed that she knew something was wrong when she found herself spraying disinfectant on her bananas. But we get it, right? Maybe we didn't spray fruit with thick peels, but we had our own attempts at protecting ourselves and our families from danger.

And it doesn't stop at a pandemic. All over the world, people are afraid. Trembling because of heights, terrorism, government corruption, public speaking, war, tight spaces, presidential election results, bridges, crime, spiders, death, change, cancer, different people and cultures, to name some common fears. Some of the fears are warranted and others are not. At the height of fear, it can be difficult to discern the difference.

What's certain is fear is prevalent in a world where evil, sin, and suffering are served on tap. There's no way around it. It's one of the aftershocks of the Fall, which means it's common to everyone—to you and to me. We feel these aftershocks radiate within our individual communities and lives. And the Bible anticipates this. That's why the most common command found on its pages is "Do not fear." God knows the waves of fear and anxiety will touch us all.

When we look at the Scriptures, we encounter a charcuterie of fears cut up and laid out for display in the lives of believers for us to ingest. Almost every patriarch in Scripture is told "not to fear," because the currents of concern flow to us all. This command reaches Abraham,[1] Isaac,[2] Jacob,[3] Moses,[4] Joshua,[5] Isaiah,[6] Jeremiah,[7] Ezekiel,[8]

---

1. Genesis 15:1
2. Genesis 26:24
3. Isaiah 43:1
4. Numbers 21:34; Deuteronomy 3:2
5. Joshua 1:3–9; 8:1; 10:8; 11:6
6. Isaiah 8:12–13
7. Jeremiah 1:8; Lamentations 3:57
8. Ezekiel 2:6; 3:9

Daniel,[9] the Disciples,[10] Mary,[11] Jairus,[12] John,[13] and even an entire church in Smyrna.[14] No matter the stage of life or position, fear and anxiety touch each of us and our communities. *What are you afraid of?*

While we are talking about how fears are common to mankind, I think this would be a good time to pause and make sure we're straight on what exactly I mean when I speak of fear and anxiety in this book.

What Is Natural Fear and Anxiety?

Using my story as an example, I experienced fear when I saw the signs warning of deer season. I experienced anxiety later, after the accident happened, when my mind was telling me that I should worry about potentially hitting another deer. The first deer existed in real time (fear), the second one did not (anxiety). I experienced trauma in my body's physiological response because of the memory my body held due to the accident. Ed Welch says it this way: "[Fear] says there is a real threat." While fear has its reasons, anxiety is less precise. It is harder to locate a specific cause,[15] and "trauma usually identifies an event that has brought death close."[16] What is tricky about fear and anxiety is there can be a mix of several things happening all at once. My mind was cloudy with these pieces, and it can be hard to make sense of it all, especially when, because of this heightened state, my mind was not able to think sharply.

Let me introduce you to an old friend who I believe helps us create some common ground around the concept of fear in particular. The Puritan John Flavel gives us three categories for fear: natural, sinful,

---

9. Daniel 10:19
10. Matthew 8:26; 10:26, 28, 31; 14:27; 17:7; Mark 4:40; 6:50; 13:7; Luke 5:10; 8:25; 12:4, 7, 32; 21:9; John 6:19–20; 14:27
11. Matthew 28:10
12. Mark 5:36; Luke 8:50
13. Revelation 1:17
14. Revelation 2:10
15. Ed Welch, *A Small Book for The Anxious Heart* (New Growth Press, 2019), Day 2.
16. Ed Welch, *PTSD and Trauma*, CCEF, May 22, 2017, https://www.ccef.org/ptsd-and-trauma.

and religious.[17] Since anxiety is a derivative of fear, I think we can glean from these categories. We've talked a bit already about sinful fear when we observed the response of Adam and Eve, and we will talk more about it later. But first, I want us to consider natural fear. Flavel says,

> *Natural fear is the trouble or perturbation of mind, from the apprehension of approaching evil, or impending danger.* The word φεθος comes from a verb* that signifies flight; this is not always sinful, but it is always the fruit and consequen[ce] of sin. Since sin entered into our nature, there is no shaking off fear.[18]

The asterisk Flavel placed after "verb" refers to the Greek word *phobéō*, which means to "put to flight," or to flee from.[19] This connects to Adam's fear when he said, "I was afraid because I was naked, so I hid." The word for "afraid" is the Hebrew verb *yare'* which primarily conveys the idea of fear, ranging from a sense of terror or dread to reverence and awe.[20] It is the Hebrew equivalent to the Greek word *phobéō*. It is when we flee or a physical response is produced within us due to us feeling inadequate or without sufficient resources. These definitions expand our view of fear since while it originates with Adam, it is not always due to personal sin but can be the result of suffering.

I want to pause for a moment and expand our categories of suffering as a believer. Flavel's definition is close to the anxiety I experienced since it did not always originate in the mind but was often the outworking of what was happening in my body. It is this type of fear that I have in mind when I speak of natural fear. There is no mention of panic or anxiety attacks in Scripture, yet they often get clumped together with sinful fear mentioned in the Bible. The closest we get to an anxiety attack is what David describes in Psalm 55:4–7 while in the thick of persecution and betrayal. He says,

---

17. John Flavel, "A Practical Treatise of Fear" in *The Whole Works of John Flavel*, Vol. 3 (London: W. Baynes and Son, 1820), 245.
18. Flavel, "A Practical Treatise of Fear," 245.
19. Strong's Lexicon, s.v. 5401 (*phóbos*) https://biblehub.com/greek/5401.htm.
20. Strong's Lexicon, s.v. 3372 (*yare'*) https://biblehub.com/hebrew/3372.htm.

My heart shudders within me;
terrors of death sweep over me.
Fear and trembling grip me;
horror has overwhelmed me.

I said, "If only I had wings like a dove!
I would fly away and find rest.
How far away I would flee;
I would stay in the wilderness. *Selah*

David is gripped by fear and trembling yet later in the psalm it is clear that he fears the Lord and continuously trusts in Him (vv. 16–19, 22–23).

If you are experiencing physical symptoms in your body and you know the feeling of being gripped by fear and trembling, I imagine you too have desired to fly away to find rest. To flee. This fear and trembling is often not the result of unbelief in God but rather a response to the real concerns as a result of sudden surges of mounting physical arousal. These can present as heart palpitations, tightening in the chest, shortness of breath, dizziness, faintness, sweating, trembling, shaking, tingling in hands and feet, abdominal distress, choking sensations, and a swirling mind. Sometimes, along with these physical sensations, is feeling the need to run away for fear of going crazy, dying, doing something uncontrollable, or being seen out of control.

When you experience these sensations, you are in the thick of the storm. Your mind and body are soaked from the terrors of the rising waters. Some of us become so discouraged because of our fears that we are constantly on the hunt for sin in our hearts. If you have been taught that if you get rid of the sin hiding within then the anxiety will also flee, you can find yourself engaged in a game of whack-a-mole. I have experienced this torment. Don't misunderstand me, we must take sin seriously. However, some of us have been taught—similar to those dealing with physical ailments—that if only we have enough faith, we will have a perfect mind and body on this side of eternity. My friend, this is a prosperity gospel, and not the gospel of Christ. Stay with me.

Helpful Fears

Have you thought about how at its core, natural fear is connected to that basic human desire to remain alive? Said another way, natural fear can be helpful and essential to our humanity because it is vital to our survival. Even though natural fear is a result of the Fall, it's also an important, hard-wired reaction that protects us from the threats of the Fall.

What do I mean? When we experience natural fear, it is a reaction, often physical, to the fact that something is wrong. Therefore, fear helps protect us and others from danger. Fear is like a fire detector telling us there is smoke in the house giving us time to escape before there is a fire. Our nervous system triggers the release of stress hormones that generate our "fight, flight, freeze, or fawn" responses, so we can minimize a very real threat. These responses help us protect ourselves and others from danger.

Let me give an example for each. If a person threatens our child, we may need to aggressively move toward that person and **fight** to protect the child. However, if a vicious dog runs toward us, we might grab our child and take **flight** to escape. If dealing with an intruder, it might be most helpful to **freeze** underneath your bed, allowing them not to notice you until they leave the house and you are safe. If you are being held captive, a **fawn** response might be a tactic to reduce abusiveness.[21] Each of these responses is a way to protect us or others from danger or lower our chances of enduring harm.

Eventually, our stress hormones will calm down once the threat has passed. However, when you throw trauma in the mix, our body sometimes experiences these triggers even after the threat is no longer active. It's like muscle memory. For example, I shared how, for many years, my brain told my body that I was in danger if I got behind the wheel of a car. This was especially likely to happen when the conditions were like they were during the accident, when I was the driver, when it was dark outside, and when I was on a turnpike. My

---

21. Fawning is often observed in those who have been lured into a cult or on the receiving end of spiritual abuse, domestic violence, or human trafficking.

fight-or-flight response activated not because my body is incapable of driving or because I didn't want to, but because my body was trying to protect me from another accident.

Many people who have been to war experience this as well. My neighbor is rarely seen without his Vietnam veteran baseball cap. One afternoon I came upon him, kneeling down, gardening with his back to me. Startled by my approach, his long sturdy body quickly bounced and landed upon his canvas sneakers as though his extremities were springs. Over four decades later, he still experiences flashbacks from his time serving. His wife later approached me apologetically and whispered to me about his time at war. From that point on, I made sure to announce myself when coming up our shared walkway.

In short, some fears are appropriate and helpful because they motivate us to avoid harm. Other times, fear is the body's memory telling our mind to be concerned. Each are there to try to help us navigate real threats in a fallen world.

The Fear of Danger

Having a healthy, natural fear of danger is a good thing. You are not necessarily in sin if you are afraid of actual threats. The fact that you react is because you have been made in the image of God and He created you to take certain precautions. We should safeguard our bodies because we are not our own, our bodies are ours to steward, they are to be cared for and protected. When we have a right view of the fear of danger, we do just that.

Not only do we need protection for our bodies, but for our spirit, and that's where fear related to spiritual dangers comes into play. We should be cautious when it comes to protecting our spiritual life. "Should we continue in sin so that grace may multiply? Absolutely not! How can we who died to sin still live in it?"[22] We run away from sin like Joseph did when he was confronted by Potiphar's wife.[23] Living a

---

22. Romans 6:1–2
23. Genesis 39

life of godliness guards us from the spiritual dangers of worldliness. We must be cautious of those things which would try to undermine our relationship with God, not only personal sin but legalism and false teaching. If we have no naturally God-given concern about our supernatural state, we will become apathetic and passive about our relationship with God. And, "what will it profit a man if he gains the whole world and forfeits his soul? Or what shall a man give in return for his soul?"[24] The answer should be: nothing. We guard our soul because it is of great value, like our bodies, given to us by God to steward. Both physical and spiritual fear of danger serve a purpose.

You may be wondering why God would make us with a propensity to be naturally afraid when He could've made us all superheroes with an "S" on our chest and a cape. But that's not the type of flying away David meant in Psalm 55. Trembling is meant to convince us of what God already knows, and we are prone to forget: We are weak and insufficient, and He is strong and all-sufficient.

Paul's Thorn in the Flesh

The apostle Paul was familiar with affliction and fears and he teaches us something about their purpose through the thorn in his flesh. Paul was given a thorn, not to destroy him but to keep him dependent upon God. We don't know the details of the thorn in Paul's flesh. He calls it a "messenger of Satan," with the purpose of torment.[25] Whether this caused physical, emotional, or spiritual torment or all the above, we don't know. But it was bad enough for him to persistently ask for God to remove it. Paul prayed three times that God would remove the thorn, and God refused. Sometimes God miraculously removes our physical or mental ailment, but in this case, God chose not to remove the thorn but to allow it to remain to make Paul humble. God's response to Paul asking God to take it away was, "My grace is sufficient for you, for my power is perfected in weakness."[26]

24. Matthew 16:26 ESV
25. 2 Corinthians 12:7
26. 2 Corinthians 12:9

Paul responds by saying that he will boast even more in his weaknesses, taking pleasure in them, so that God's power would reside in him.[27] True strength comes from God when we acknowledge our weakness. Boasting in our weakness with God in view doesn't lead us to condemnation, it leads us to glory in our God and His power.[28]

If we, like Paul, have asked God to take a thorn in our flesh away, and He has chosen not to, it must mean that God has a plan greater than ours. God wants to expose our weakness and neediness so that we might look to Him for that which we lack. If God will not change our anxiety, then He must want to change us and how we relate to our anxiety. He uses this thorn in our flesh to accomplish His purposes.

Paul didn't throw up his hands and say, "Well, until this thorn vanishes, I will not continue in my calling and my ministry." Nor did he conclude that the presence of the thorn meant that he did not believe or that he needed to root out the source of some hidden sin. Instead, he moved forward in his calling and ministry *while* the thorn was still in his side. About a year earlier he communicated to the church: "I came to you *in weakness with great fear and trembling*."[29] Paul's entire ministry was marked with affliction. He didn't wait for the trembling to pass. For those of us whose thorn is anxiety, we would do well to follow his example. Rather than condemn ourselves, we can know that these afflictions do not always mean sin. C. S. Lewis said,

> Some people feel guilty about their anxieties and regard them as a defect of faith but they are afflictions, not sins. Like all afflictions, they are, if we can so take them, our share in the Passion of Christ.[30]

This doesn't mean we don't tend to the wound in our side. It doesn't mean we ignore anxiety and just press on like a machine. The goal may initially be to pray and ask God to get the thorn out of our

---

27. 2 Corinthians 12:9–10
28. 2 Corinthians 10:17–18
29. 1 Corinthians 2:3 NIV, emphasis added
30. C. S. Lewis, *Letters to Malcolm: Chiefly on Prayer* (Harcourt Brace Jovanovich, 1964), 41.

flesh. However, if the Father responds with "my grace is sufficient for you,"[31] we know that God will meet us in our weakness and adversity.

So, the question is not "Why do we have fear?"—we know the origin. The questions is, "Now that fear is here, what is God trying to produce in us through the affliction of anxiety?" I am convinced that according to the Scripture above, it is more of Christ's power in us. God works not as we would. In God's kingdom, the way up is down, and the way to strength is through acknowledging our weakness, and the way to Christ sometimes means we are met with fearful things. This reminds me of a hymn by the English poet and hymnwriter William Cowper who, throughout his life, had a thorn of deep depression and periods of mental illness thought to be bipolar II disorder. He wrote the song, "God Moves in a Mysterious Way."

Verse 1
God moves in a mysterious way,
His wonders to perform.
He plants his footsteps in the sea
And rides upon the storm.
Deep in the dark and hidden mines,
With never-failing skill,
He fashions all his bright designs
And works his sov'reign will.

Refrain
So God we trust in you.
O God, we trust in you.
When tears are great and comforts few,
We hope in mercies ever new,
We trust in you.

Verse 2
Oh, fearful saints, new courage take:
The clouds that you now dread
Are big with mercy and will break

31. 2 Corinthians 12:9

In blessings on your head.
Judge not the Lord by feeble sense,
But trust him for his grace
Behind a frowning providence,
He hides a smiling face.

Verse 3
God's purposes will ripen fast,
Unfolding every hour.
The bud may have a bitter taste,
But sweet will be the flower.
Blind unbelief is sure to err
And scan his work in vain.
God is his own interpreter,
And he will make it plain.[32]

Fear and anxiety are mysterious to us but plain to God. We often do not understand why we are to suffer so greatly with these cares, thorns, and terrors. Like Paul, we can ask God to take them away, and He may, but if He doesn't, we can trust that He will make His purpose plain in His time.

I want you to know there is a purpose for you in your storm. No matter how you ended up in this raging sea, it is one common to us all, and not one drop of this mysterious water is in vain.

32. William Cowper, "God Moves in a Mysterious Way," (1774). Public domain.

CHAPTER 4

When Fear Is a Snare

In C. S. Lewis's *The Screwtape Letters*, we get a glimpse into how the devil tempts us to view fear. If you're not familiar, in the novel, the "Enemy" is God, and "Screwtape" is an old devil, writing letters to his nephew, the young devil, "Wormwood." Screwtape trains Wormwood on how to tempt the Christian assigned to him. The Christian is being called to military service. Screwtape tells Wormwood that one of the best ways to tempt is to get him to focus his attention on the uncertainties surrounding the future so that he is filled with anxieties. He wants this man to be consumed by his fears about the future but never able to identify them so that he cannot discern that these fears are a tribulation from God to draw his attention to God. Screwtape tells Wormwood to keep the man focused upon doing good works toward others so he forgets who he is doing them for. Then all his virtues become outward rather than inward, making the reason why he is engaging in charity a complete fantasy.[1]

We can be very much like this Christian man, though we often do not realize it; we can get caught up in debilitating fears that have been set as a trap for us. The Bible tells us that the fear of man is a snare.[2] A snare is a hidden trap on the ground covered with leaves and twigs disguising the plan. The enemy convinces us that all our attention should be on our fears rather than on our God. As we believe this lie, the things that we do slowly go from being done for God's eyes to

1. C. S. Lewis, *The Screwtape Letters* (Centenary Press, 1945), 34–38.
2. Proverbs 29:25

being done for the eyes of others. Before we know it, we are captured in a net hanging by our feet.

Sinful Fear

The problem is not that we experience fear in our life, since we have established that it can be quite natural. The problem, then, is when we replace fear *for* our life, when it keeps us from the One who *is* our Life by drawing our attention to our fear as though it sits on the throne rather than our Holy God.

Our friend Flavel calls sinful fear a fear that carnal and unbelieving men have when dangers threaten. This fear flows from unbelief and an unworthy distrust of God.[3] The New Testament describes sinful fear as "worry" or "anxiousness" by the Greek word *merimna*, which means to care to the point where one is divided or separated into parts.[4] Your attention is divided and all your devotion is diverted to worry. The worst form of this, from the Bible's perspective, is to not revere God. One way we do not rightly revere God is through the fear of man.

Fear of Man

What is the fear of man? It is minimizing our trust in God and magnifying our trust in man, including in ourselves. This fear magnifies the creature, since man's position increases and God's position as the Creator, decreases. It comes with an attempt to gain the praise, approval, or good opinions of other people and ourselves. We put human opinion above the security of God's intelligence and Divine promise. The most famous teaching by Jesus, which gets at our heart

3. John Flavel, "A Practical Treatise of Fear" in *The Whole Works of John Flavel*, Vol. 3 (London: W. Baynes and Son, 1820), 248.

4. Strong's Lexicon, s.v. 3309 (*merimnaó*), https://biblehub.com/greek/3309.htm. It's important to note that the earliest English translations of the Bible do not have the word "anxiety" in them. Where our modern translations use "anxiety," the Tyndale translation says, "Be not car[e]ful," and the KJV says, "be careful for nothing."

on this matter, is in the Sermon on the Mount (spoiler alert: It tells us at the end, "do not worry").

> "Be careful not to practice your righteousness in front of others ***to be seen by them***. Otherwise, you have no reward with your Father in heaven. So whenever you give to the poor, don't sound a trumpet before you, as the hypocrites do in the synagogues and on the streets, ***to be applauded by people***. Truly I tell you, they have their reward. But when you give to the poor, don't let your left hand know what your right hand is doing, so that your giving may be in secret. And your Father who sees in secret will reward you. Whenever you pray, you must not be like the hypocrites, because they love to pray standing in the synagogues and on the street corners ***to be seen by people***. Truly I tell you, they have their reward. But when you pray, go into your private room, shut your door, and pray to your Father who is in secret. And your Father who sees in secret will reward you. When you pray, don't babble like the Gentiles, since ***they imagine they'll be heard for their many words***. Don't be like them, because your Father knows the things you need before you ask him. . . . Whenever you fast, don't be gloomy like the hypocrites. For they disfigure their faces so that their fasting is ***obvious to people***. Truly I tell you, they have their reward. But when you fast, put oil on your head and wash your face, so that your fasting isn't obvious to others but to your Father who is in secret. And your Father who sees in secret will reward you."[5]

Jesus is critical of the religious leaders of His day. Why? Because they engage in pious activity, not to show love and reverence to God

5. Matthew 6:1–8, 16–18, emphasis added

while helping the needy, but to boast in themselves and be recognized by other people. Like the videos that often circulate today of people giving money to others while making sure to record the exchange and upload it online for likes and to go viral. Activities like giving to the poor, praying, and fasting are only godly acts when they are done in the name of God and out of reverence for God. But when the motive is to be seen, heard, and applauded by others, it is not at all about God.

The fear of man makes for a terrible god. It is the worst tyrant a person can live under. Public opinion sways like wind hitting a lone leaf. It blows you from north to west, east to south. It is never satisfied. Our own insecurity and the constant demands of other people constantly shifts the needle. There will always be a person more impressive than you. And even if you get to be the most impressive person in the room, the room will shift and the glory that comes with it lasts for only a few minutes. Eventually, the scene changes and you enter a different room. You could have wowed the board room in your financial presentation, but eventually, you have to come through the front door and be a parent (and we all know our kids are not wowed with us for long!). Even more important, we may be impressive in earthly rooms but if God is unimpressed when we walk though His gates, does the praise we received in this life really matter?

Approval, if it's not given by God, is like clipped flowers. You enjoy the bouquet in its pretty vase. Others may comment about the pleasant fragrance and vibrant petals, but it's already technically dead. Its beauty is short-lived. Soon the flowers will darken, mold, let off a stench, and the petals will begin to fall.

The fear of man gets especially lethal when it sets itself not just on the favor of another person, but on the *position* of someone else—especially when this person already has the mass approval you're longing for. This is jealousy or covetousness. The logic goes like this: *I want the approval of the masses, but you have it instead of me, so I'll do whatever it takes to cast you down so that I might rise and be the object of everyone's admiration.* A biblical example of this is King Saul, who was "afraid" of

David.[6] First Samuel 18 shows the contrast between Saul and David. A couple of chapters earlier God rejected Saul as king because of his refusal to obey God concerning the Amalekites. God has Samuel anoint David who, based upon appearances, seems least likely to be king since he was a shepherd and outwardly not as impressive as Saul. Despite this, God uses David to defeat Goliath (ultimately pointing to Jesus who will defeat Satan). Saul notices David's success and overhears a song celebrating David for his victory in battle: "Saul has killed his thousands, but David his tens of thousands."[7]

If we follow the story in 1 Samuel 1:8–15, Saul resents David and tries to destroy him from that day forward. He sets what he thinks will be a trap to kill David, by requiring him to present a dowry of 100 Philistine foreskins to marry his daughter. David successfully fulfills the task times two, leaving Saul fuming because God is allowing David to have success in all his endeavors. This contempt for David's success causes Saul to fear David and hate him. "Saul realized that the LORD was with David and that his daughter Michal loved him, and ***he became even more afraid of David. As a result, Saul was David's enemy from then on.***"[8]

The fear of man—whether fearing a person or position—breeds hatred, anxious toil, and tempts us to disobey God's command to love God and our neighbor. The fear of man exchanges love for God with the love of man, which below the surface is a love of self. It also replaces the love of our neighbor with the love of self since one cannot live out the command to love others unless we are genuinely trusting God for our needs of approval and success. For when we rejoice when our neighbor receives praise or success, it shows that our identity is rooted in God and not our insecurities. When their success causes us to hate and fear, we are wrongly comparing ourselves to that person and are worshipping an idol of position and/or success. When we trust in the God who delivers us and encourages us in our gospel identity, we no

---

6. 1 Samuel 18:12
7. 1 Samuel 18:7
8. 1 Samuel 18:28–29, emphasis added

longer live our lives yoked to the opinions of people but freely live out God's call, as stated in the Sermon on the Mount.

To Revere Thine Own Self

In a desperate desire to regain control of our environment, we revere or fear ourselves. What do I mean by fearing yourself? To recall what we learned in chapter 3: Biblically fearing something in the sinful sense means to assign too much weight to a thing or overly care because we feel inadequate or without sufficient resources. The problem with fearing self is that we think the answer is in our ability to handle a situation that we don't have the resources for. So, when you fear yourself in the middle of an anxiety wave, you are essentially assigning to yourself all the weight and responsibility of making it stop. When you size up anxiety and then size up yourself, you consider yourself a heavyweight champ against it. You may not consciously think you will win, but the unwillingness to cast over the fear to God shows that, even subconsciously, you think you can outmaneuver it or control it in various ways. But if my experience has anything to say to that, you won't and you can't. Trust me, I've tried.

Terrifying Voices

We already saw how the enemy can have a terrifying voice by distorting the truth and saying things like, in the garden, "Did God really say?"[9] But there are times when the terrifying voice comes not from an enemy but a dear companion. Like Peter, who denied that Jesus would suffer, be killed, and raised on the third day. Peter responded, saying, "Oh no, Lord! This will never happen to you!" Jesus turned and told Peter, "Get behind me, Satan! You are a hindrance to me because you're not thinking about God's concerns but human concerns."[10] Jesus was not swayed by Peter, but often we are swayed by the voices of people in our lives that we love.

9. Genesis 3:1
10. Matthew 16:22–23

One example of this I have been able to see is in my relationship with my mother. I first identified my mother-wounds after leaving an abusive church. My mother loved me, yet as a young, single mother, she struggled with control. To counteract her grappling with her life choices, she put extremely high expectations of her American dream on her children. This meant that I was primarily praised when I accomplished goals and achievements that advanced her dream, and I was punished or harshly reprimanded for small mistakes. This experience trickled into my relationship with God, myself, and others. I struggled hearing God's voice over hers.

Once I became a Christian, that dominant voice transferred from my mother to a toxic pastor. He used his words to manipulate and spiritually abuse the sheep. He created unrealistic expectations for the church and his voice often contradicted God's. At times, I accepted his words despite my discernment telling me otherwise. Once I began to grow in the Lord, I began going against his voice to obey God's voice. It took years to get his voice and other toxic voices, including my own, out of my head. Parent, pastor, or otherwise, these prominent personalities can cause anxiety when you want to follow God's will for your life. When we are afraid of the authority figures in our lives, we often quiet God to appease them. This is another way we can fear man.

For so long, I toiled, trying to take a fly swatter to every voice I heard buzzing around my head. Sometimes I succeeded, other times their voices were still too loud—like buzzing flies. I was swatting, but they were still whispering and swarming. Over time, I realized that the more familiar I made myself with God's voice, the quieter those other voices became. I also realized that, as Psalm 81 reveals, God *wants* me to listen to Him not just for my own sanity, but for my good and my satisfaction:

> Hear, O my people, while I admonish you! . . . But my people did not ***listen to my voice;*** Israel would not submit to me. So I gave them over to their stubborn hearts, to follow *their own counsels*. Oh, that my people would ***listen to me,*** that Israel would walk in my ways! I would soon subdue their enemies . . . [I]

> would feed you with the finest of the wheat, and with honey from the rock I would satisfy you."[11]

God's voice must grow louder and more familiar if harmful voices are to hush. Once we learn how to discern the voices which align with God's Word, we will have clarity. As we grow in maturity and discernment, we will experience what the Bible promises: "Whether you turn to the right or to the left, your ears will *hear a voice* behind you, saying, 'This is the way; walk in it.'"[12] The Bible makes clear: "Fearing people is a dangerous trap, but trusting the LORD means safety."[13] That safety exists even if no one else in the world praises you for it; we can hold fast to the promises of God, knowing they are sure.

Do Not Worry

When Jesus taught about the difference between the righteous and the hypocrite and how they are to approach giving, praying, and fasting, He says to the disciples,

> "No one can serve two masters, since either he will hate one and love the other, or he will be devoted to one and despise the other. You cannot serve both God and money. Therefore I tell you: Don't worry about your life, what you will eat or what you will drink; or about your body, what you will wear. Isn't life more than food and the body more than clothing?"[14]

What Jesus is saying here is that the righteous give their possessions not hypocritically but freely and quietly to the poor and/or to their enemies out of love and faith. They need not worry about their clothes, because they can freely give their coat to the one who sues them to go the extra mile of displaying Christian charity.[15] The

11. Psalm 81:8, 11–14, 16 ESV, emphasis added
12. Isaiah 30:21 NIV, emphasis added
13. Proverbs 29:25 NLT
14. Matthew 6:24–25
15. Matthew 5:40–42

righteous pray, not hypocritically standing on the corner to be seen, but quietly, forgiving offenses and clearing the debts of others done against them before God, knowing they have been forgiven and will receive true rewards.[16] The righteous fast, not hypocritically or to make it seem obvious to others, but privately for God, to lament the absence of Christ's presence after His resurrection and ascension.[17]

This is why Jesus talks about food, drink, and clothes when He says not to worry since these are practical things that they would lose because of their commitment to follow Christ. I don't think Jesus is saying if a person is in need of basic necessities, they should not be concerned, or if they ask for help, they are worrying and therefore not trusting God. I don't believe Jesus has basic necessities in mind, which is why He says, "The Gentiles eagerly seek all these things."[18] If these were basic necessities, wouldn't everyone be seeking them? Jesus is not saying the financially poor should not worry, but the poor in spirit should not, because the kingdom of heaven belongs to them.[19] God's kingdom reality impacts how we see our afflictions.

Jesus is saying this: Practice righteousness. Suffer for the right motives. Live out the heart of the law and you will show that you are blessed by God, even if the world does not think so. The hypocritical here are those who are worrying and storing up earthly treasures. They are those who are divided. Recall, we talked about the word *merimna,* which means to care to the point where one is divided or separated into parts.[20] That is what is used here in place of the words *worry* or *anxious*. Here, the division being referred to is trying to serve God *and* money.

Jesus is not saying that we will never have any anxieties. He is saying if you are suffering for righteousness' sake, you ultimately don't have to worry. You can seek first the kingdom of God and His righteousness, and even if you suffer you can know that your ultimate needs have been provided. This doesn't mean we will not suffer. This

16. Matthew 6:9–13
17. Matthew 9:14–15
18. Matthew 6:32
19. Matthew 5:3
20. *Strong's Lexicon*, s.v. 3309 (*merimnaó*) https://biblehub.com/greek/3309.htm.

is a *guarantee* that we will suffer. There is an ultimate kingdom we are living for. God will care for His children as they suffer with Him.[21] As we take on this suffering, we must not forget our God-given identity as salt and light; we must be faithful to the point of death[22] because our good works amid tribulation point ourselves and others to the glory of God.[23] We do not do these acts to make ourselves righteous or to be esteemed by others.[24] We do them because Christ has already made us righteous by faith to do good works God ordained for us.[25] The Beatitudes remind us of the kingdom reality we have attained by faith regardless of how we fear or feel.

We may be tempted to think that someone who seems to never struggle with fear—someone who appears, bold, and shows outward displays of piety—is righteous. Jesus reminds us again that God sees our hearts. Those who may be in the spotlight, seeking or receiving the affirmation of men, may be divided with motives full of fear, while those who are trembling show by faith that they are obedient, a crumbly claystone pot filled with eternal treasure.[26] The Pharisees' desire for the spotlight made them jealous of the one who was jealous for them. The only one who could save them from their fear-induced snare was Jesus. And save many of them He did. Some Pharisees followed Jesus and walked in faith, casting off that internal division to wholeheartedly follow their Prince of Peace.

This Prince tells us that we are not to boast in our abilities but ask, seek, and knock.[27] Christians are recognized not by our strength but by our Savior's strength and the good fruit the Spirit produces in us.[28] Revisiting the Sermon on the Mount doesn't condemn those of us dealing with anxiety and panic attacks, but encourages the righteous, regardless if they are anxious or not, because it reminds us that we are

21. Matthew 7:7–11
22. Revelation 2:10
23. Matthew 5:13–16
24. Matthew 7:21–23
25. Ephesians 2:8–10
26. 2 Corinthians 4:7–12
27. Matthew 7:7
28. Matthew 7:17

not divided on the King and kingdom we are anticipating.[29] In Christ, He takes our weaknesses and carries our diseases, including anxiety.[30] Even when our body shakes, if we have built our trembling life upon the Rock, we will never ultimately be shaken.[31]

We must not allow the snare of the fear of man to trip us up from beholding the greatness of our God. That is exactly what Wormwood wants us to do. We are not divided, so we will not submit to devils but to our God.

29. Matthew 6:33
30. Matthew 4:24
31. Matthew 7:24

CHAPTER 5

He Seeks Us

My husband and I have a child who fears sleeping alone and often asks to sleep with us in our bed. The fear is there, but lying next to us brings great comfort. If your kids are anything like my child, this act of sleeping with Mommy and Daddy helps them focus more on you and your ability to protect them than their internal angst.

Perhaps you, like us, encourage your kids to sleep in their bed on their own when the situation isn't all that dire. But when it *is* dire—when they are inconsolable, when there's some sort of real danger, or when they wake up in the middle of the night screaming with night terrors—perhaps you, like us, snap out of bed and run toward them. Perhaps you lay with them for a few minutes to help with the transition back to sleep, assuring them that if there is an intruder, storm, fire, or boogie man, you are near and will do everything in your power to protect them. Whether it's in the middle of the night or otherwise, when white-hot fear kicks in, there's something kids feel when their parent seeks them out in the middle of that fear. Safe. Secure. Protected. Everything opposite of anxious.

Fear Tells Us We Can Be like God

When we feel afraid or anxious, hunkering near the one you trust is good. The problem is when you find your security and trust in an untrustworthy source. Recalling chapter 2, we looked at how Satan deceived Adam and Eve by twisting God's words in a way that caused them to doubt God's character and intentions.

> "No! You will certainly not die," the serpent said to the woman. "In fact, God knows that when you eat it your eyes will be opened and you will be like God, knowing good and evil."[1]

When Satan said, "Your eyes would be opened," the enemy brought attention to the fact that despite all God allowed Adam and Eve to see, they were shortsighted because they did not see and know the difference between good and evil. They were innocent in the best way possible, knowing only good, unfamiliar with evil, and unable to recognize the cunning ways of the serpent or the fact that they were naked. Yet, after talking with the serpent, they wanted to be like God, to see much more, to understand what good and evil meant. They wanted to have haughty eyes—eyes to behold things too lofty and too difficult for them to process.[2]

While God knows all the possibilities of evil, because of His holiness, He never indulges in it and is always distinct from it. He understands how evil works, but unlike humans, He is unable to be corrupted by it, and He has the divine power to fix it. However, if you've ever witnessed something traumatic, you know what it is to behold evil you never should have seen. Seeing evil at its worst was not a burden God meant for humans to carry. Likewise, not just to witness evil but to know it to the point of carrying it out yourself in various ways is also something God never meant for humans to experience.

Satan's promise of experiencing opened eyes was another way of saying, "You'll know something you didn't know before. You'll become familiar with something only God understands and has the power to handle." Said a different way, to truly see something is to know it on an experiential level. This is why, when we have a deeply encouraging chat with a friend or counselor, we say things like, "For the first time, I felt seen." We don't mean they simply beheld us with their eyes. We mean, they *get* us. Satan's promise was this: *When your eyes are opened, you'll understand not just good, which is something you're used to, but*

1. Genesis 3:4–5
2. Psalm 131:1

something else that God is holding you back from knowing—evil. You already know how good works, but you could know more. You could know how evil works, too. God already knows this—why can't you? Why would He limit you from knowing the whole picture instead of just one part? Don't you want to be like God?

With that question came great fear—Adam and Eve had FOMO: fear of missing out. Fear of not being able to know it all and have it all. The devil convinced them that God was keeping something from them, and they felt they needed to know about evil and good themselves. They did not understand that this unfamiliarity with evil was a mercy. They were good and wanted that which was good—to innocently be like God. Yet they listened to Satan because they were unfamiliar with evil and didn't understand the consequences. Immediately their world shifted. They sought resources outside of their good Creator. They believed the devil's trick. They rebelled against God and were left with subsequent fear and anxiety. They then attempted to cover up the whole ordeal with fig leaves.

Once the door was opened to evil, a crater crashed between humanity and God, fracturing everything. As a result of listening to the devil, humanity would experience the consequence of their sin: divine judgment. The promised penalty for breaking God's law was not just exposure, but death. They exchanged life for the "king of terrors."[3] They trusted in the devil's lies when he said, "No! You will certainly not die."[4] Yet they *would* die. They were convinced by the serpent that they could live a life apart from the one who is their Life. The tree seemed pleasant and good to eat even though God told them it was to be avoided at all costs. Satan deceived them into believing that they could live lives enjoying created things without obeying their Creator.

3. Job 18:14; Proverbs 7:27
4. Genesis 3:4

Found by God When Fear Is Due to Sin

There are two kinds of death resulting from the Fall: physical and spiritual. The physical curse of death would not happen immediately—but it was only a matter of time before they would feel the fullness of its sting. One day, they'd be buried, going right back into the ground from which they were formed.[5] In a spiritual sense, though, from the moment the forbidden fruit was eaten, a sort of death happened immediately between mankind and God. The perfect and unfiltered relationship they had with Him was now torn. They had to be driven out of His presence, exiled from the garden, for they were no longer fit for that place.[6] Evil cannot coexist with holiness. Where there was once a perfect bond, they were then cut off from God. They knew only daylight before, but now they were getting familiar with the terrors of the night. They were covered in guilt and shame, as the glory of God that had shone on them was now dull. Their light was replaced with darkness. Glory was replaced with nakedness, immortality with mortality. I suppose they got what they wanted, for now they knew what evil felt like, and had their eyes opened to its consequences. Just imagine how hard that was. The constant memory of Eden before the Fall. The constant reminder of hard work and toil after having had it easier and better. Better still, the memory of the holy joy they experienced in fellowship with God. Oh, how far they'd fallen.

The fear of missing out turned into even deeper fears: fear of exposure, fear of judgment, fear of new threats in a cruel and evil world, and ultimately, fear of death. These are the fears which caused them to hide from God and to cover themselves up with fig leaves. Yet, as we touched on before, despite their fear, failure, and flailing, we find that God not only upholds His promise of death but also makes a way to extend mercy to them. He makes a way to cover them when their flimsy cover-up fails. Right in the middle of their sin and fears, they were met with God's presence and mercy. Right in the middle of this

5. Genesis 3:19
6. Genesis 3:23–24

new terror of the night, like any good parent does, God drew near to them.

Adam and Eve were lost like the prodigal son in Luke 15 wasting his father's inheritance in foolish living and sin. Once he realizes his error, he is determined to return home to his father. As he was still far off, the father saw him, ran toward him, and kissed him, rejoicing that the son who was lost was now found. That father clothes his son. Similarly, God cries out for Adam and Eve, "Where are you?"[7] He meets them in their shame and covers them with His abundant mercy. How kind is that? God moves toward them like a mother toward her infant who she quickly embraces and swaddles. Right in the middle of the mess they got themselves in—and their anxious response of hiding—God moved toward them. God's response to their hiding was to seek them out and directly address their fig leaves. And He does so in a certain way.

Here's the good news that we're about to see: God doesn't berate them for responding in fear and He doesn't strip them of clothing so that they stand naked and ashamed. No, God has a better plan to cover them with something far greater. More than that, He removes the entire reason they feel anxious to begin with. God is not caught off guard by this whole situation. This plan of redemption was God's intent before He created anything.[8] Their fall from glory was an opportunity for God to lavish them with His kindness, and so He did.

God's Answer to Our Sin, Our Anxiety, and Our Greatest Fear

How did God do it? What was this "far greater" answer from heaven that could cover their exposure and soothe their greatest fear? There are three answers: a stronger covering, a better tree, and a greater Adam who steps into our world and succeeds where the first Adam failed.

7. Genesis 3:9
8. Revelation 13:8

A Stronger Covering

What does God use in place of those fig leaves? "The LORD God made clothing from animal skins for Adam and his wife."[9]

All of humanity needs an exchange of clothes. We need God to remove our rags and replace them with righteous robes. But why animal skins? What's happening here, and what is it trying to point us toward? Eden was once a space completely unfamiliar with death. But after the Fall, the first death was the spiritual death of Adam and Eve and the second death was the physical death of an animal. Why this second act of death? To atone for Adam and Eve's spiritual death. Because sin brought death, God required that an animal must die to atone for the breaking of God's law. God provides the sacrificial animal because "without the shedding of blood there is no forgiveness" of sin.[10]

Adam and Eve were sin-filled, shaking, and afraid. Their anxious responses get them nowhere close to a real solution. God, on the other hand, has a solution in mind. He cried out for them, intentionally seeking them out to restore the relational fray and clothe them with His mercy by means of atonement. Their sin, shame, and anxieties would be covered satisfactorily. The animal's death pointed toward the new way God would tell His people to handle sin—at least for a time—and that was through animal sacrifice.

Ultimately, Christians know an atonement much greater than the one in Genesis 3. What God did for Adam and Eve was a foreshadowing of what He would do through Jesus Christ, the Lamb of God, once and for all time. God has undoubtedly cried out for us, for we would never discern or desire Him unless He drew near to us first.[11] Then, in mercy, He clothed us with His Son's righteousness and met us with His presence. How did He clothe us? After a lifetime of walking in perfect obedience to the Father, our Savior Christ took on our nakedness, shame, and death through the most shameful means: crucifixion.

9. Genesis 3:21 NLT
10. Hebrews 9:22
11. John 6:44

> For you know that you were redeemed from your empty way of life inherited from your ancestors, not with perishable things like silver or gold, but with the precious blood of Christ, like that of an unblemished and spotless lamb.[12]

Jesus is the holy sacrifice that God uses as the means to justify His church. Jesus's body is not just better, but a forever-sufficient offering because Jesus was divine and human. Since Adam was human, it was required that there be an individual who could satisfy God's law by perfectly upholding and obeying God's command. An ordinary man would not be able to fulfill this since all men are born with a sin nature. It would take a sacrifice that could undo man's rebellious works while satisfying God's righteous wrath. A mere man, or an unblemished animal, would not be able to do this. It would take one who was both God *and* man to undo the sin and suffering we've endured from the Fall. It would take one who was able to perfectly keep God's law, remain morally innocent, and, as a blameless man, substitute for sinful men by taking on sin He had not committed. This is why Jesus is the Lamb of God. He alone has the resources to fulfill the law and bring all the sinful and suffering saints out of hiding.

The atonement paid by Jesus Christ for our sins on the cross of Calvary, along with His resurrection, changes everything about our lives since it removes our greatest fear of judgment by granting us peace with God. In this way, we no longer relate to Adam and Eve trembling in the garden before God clothed them. We have security in Christ because of His perfect sacrifice. We are free from the condemnation they experienced. "Perfect love drives out fear."[13] We have received a great exchange. Our sins were placed upon Christ, and His righteousness now covers us. What do I mean by "righteousness"? I mean that Christ's lifetime of walking in perfect obedience to the Father is the very record we inherit when we believe in Him! What a trade. Our record of sinful living for His record of perfect living. Our sinful fig

---

12. 1 Peter 1:18–19
13. 1 John 4:18

leaves for the perfect, radiant robe of our Savior. Our fear of judgment is replaced with peace with God.[14] When the Bible talks about white robes Christians have received, this is precisely what it is referring to.[15] Those white robes, free from the stain of sin, are a visual of the justifying work of Christ on our behalf. We are now clothed in Christ.

A Better Tree

There is another detail in the story of the Fall that we should not miss, and that's the presence of a tree. The tree from which Adam and Eve ate was a forbidden tree. Through their interaction with this tree, they ushered in sin, suffering, and death. Through a better tree—the tree at Calvary that was fashioned into a cross—Jesus died to bring salvation, sanctification, and life. Calvary was where "the God of our ancestors raised up Jesus, whom you had murdered by hanging him on a tree."[16] And what did He do on that tree? "He himself bore our sins in his body on the tree; so that, having died to sins, we might live for righteousness."[17] At a tree, Adam committed sin in his body. On a better tree, Jesus who did not know sin became sin for us. A tree was the vehicle for sin's arrival, and it is the vehicle for its removal.

Let us not miss a final contrast between the two trees: We mentioned the hiding that came with the Tree of the Knowledge of Good and Evil, along with the attempt to cover up. However, Jesus was nailed to Calvary's tree completely exposed, naked, showing His complete vulnerability and willingness to bear our shame. Ultimately, God removes the worst effects of the Fall in this way: The tree Adam ate from opened mankind's eyes to evil. The tree Jesus died on opened mankind's eyes to good. Adam's tree ushered in death, and Jesus's tree ushered in eternal life. Adam's tree was where mankind's penalty for sin started. Jesus's tree is where mankind's penalty for sin was paid in full. Adam's tree is forbidden and leads to separation from God, but at Jesus's tree, all are welcome to come and receive right standing

---

14. Romans 5:1
15. Revelation 3:5; 7:9, 13–14; Revelation 22:14
16. Acts 5:30
17. 1 Peter 2:24

with God. God takes details of the Fall—even down to a tree—and redeems them so that we might be covered, safe, and welcomed in His eternal kingdom.

A Greater Adam Enters Our World

A stronger covering (the righteousness of Christ) and a better tree (the cross at Calvary) are our only hope—but they cannot be grasped or even possible if there's no Messiah to begin with. If Jesus was never born, we'd still be waiting for some sort of solution to the human condition of sin, and all the anxious aftermath that comes with it.

The author Toni Morrison said, "Can't nothing heal without pain, you know."[18] Yes, we know, Toni. Jesus teaches us this when He stepped into our world to bear the pains of being a human in a sin-filled world to bring healing to His creation. Jesus doesn't just look down from His throne in heaven to find us in our weak state. Jesus *joins* us in our condition of human weakness.[19] His presence exposes the real wounds in our world, and His life addresses them so that through His sacrificial death, He might solve the problem of sin, bringing healing to the pain animal sacrifices could never fully cure.

Humanity's first representative, Adam, failed. What humanity needed was a new and greater Adam than the first. And that's exactly who Jesus is. Where Adam failed, Jesus conquered. He is the final and victorious Adam. This is why Romans 5:15–17 says,

> But the gift is not like the trespass. For if by the one man's trespass the many died, how much more have the grace of God and the gift which comes through the grace of the one man Jesus Christ overflowed to the many. And the gift is not like the one man's sin, because from one sin came the judgment, resulting in condemnation, but from many trespasses came the gift, resulting in justification. If by the one man's trespass, death reigned through that one man, how much

18. Toni Morrison, *Beloved* (Vintage, 2004), 92.
19. 2 Corinthians 13:4; Hebrews 4:15; 5:2

> more will those who receive the overflow of grace and the gift of righteousness reign in life through the one man, Jesus Christ.

Consider those words: "The gift is not like the trespass." We all are familiar with the results of trespassing because it's why we are suffering now. But the gift is different. The free gift of God has come to us not based on our merit or our ability to maintain a state of serenity. God came to us through Jesus to rescue us right where we were amid our chaos. The Fall's effect is all around us and in us. The gift, then, is so much greater because not only does it provide grace, which delivers us from the penalty of sin, but it also restrains us from the power of sin and will eventually save us from the presence of sin.

Hope Amid Suffering

Unfortunately, the gift of salvation does not mean that we will not suffer once we come to know Jesus, but it means that what the gift affords us has a more potent impact than the trespass ever could. The gift is more significant because not only does it deliver us from sin, it gives us hope in the middle of our suffering. This hope does not mean that this suffering will all vanish immediately. At one time, I didn't think Christians could struggle with mental health. I thought, at the moment of conversion, all of our swirling cares that move in like fog would be wiped away by a big Jesus squeegee. But the mist can persist as a constant lingering condensation. Maybe some people have had that immediate experience of being victorious over anxiety in a moment. Their fears and anxieties all dissipated overnight. However, I suspect that the vast majority of us, living in an imperfect world with an imperfect body while being sanctified over time, will have to learn tools over time that help us cling to our perfect God while we journey *with* anxiety. Faithfulness while trembling. Our great hope is that no matter where we are in our individual path—whether we feel peace in our body or war—as the storm clouds hang above us and follow us with showers that feel more like a firehose, we have a great and glorious peace with our God who stepped out of heaven to pursue us. He is well acquainted with all our ways. Psalm 139:7–12 says,

> Where can I go to escape your Spirit?
> Where can I flee from your presence?
> If I go up to heaven, you are there;
> if I make my bed in Sheol, you are there.
> If I fly on the wings of the dawn
> and settle down on the western horizon,
> even there your hand will lead me;
> your right hand will hold on to me.
> If I say, "Surely the darkness will hide me,
> and the light around me will be night"—
> even the darkness is not dark to you.
> The night shines like the day;
> darkness and light are alike to you.

Or, if we wanted to add our own anxious lyrics to these, it might sound something like:

> Where can I escape your Spirit?
> Where can I flee from Your presence?
> If *my mind swirls where concerns do not end*
> If *my heart cannot find rest from the terrors of the night.*
> If *my body trembles like an aged hand and I end up in the ER once more;*
> Even there Your hand will lead me;
> Your right hand will hold on to me.
> If I say, "Surely the darkness *of anxiety* will hide me,
> And the light around me will be night"—
> Even the darkness is not dark to You.
> The night shines like the day;
> Darkness and light are alike to You.
> If I hit another deer, even then, Your hand will lead me.

Here in our own rendition of Psalm 139, our Yahweh finds us and places Himself with us. No matter how high or low anxiety takes us. Even in the face of death or the fear of death. He seeks and finds us. Our God seeks His own. He proved His seeking knows no limits by entering our world as the Second Adam, and He proves it every day since then through His indwelling Spirit.

Christ Is Where Our Hope Resides

I don't know what you're anxious about—and there are a great many very real and terrible things that trigger our anxiety in this life. Whatever it is, I'm sure it's got a perfectly understandable origin story. But the good news for you is this: You weren't the one representative of mankind who made the one choice that literally ruined the world and cast millions of souls down the path of death. Whatever it is you're anxious about, it's real and valid, but it's not *that.* It's not Adam-level bad. And its aftermath cannot possibly be as bad as his decision was. So let me encourage you: If God can seek Adam—the most guilt-laden and fearful man on the planet—if He can bring him out of his hiding, cover him, soothe him, and beckon him into safety, He can do the same for you. If Adam, who was quite literally in a situation that truly met the requirements for "end of the world," could allow God to lovingly clothe him in a sacrificial covering, so can you. Consider: If God has taken care of the deepest and darkest anxieties of mankind when it comes to how He solved the Fall, how much more trustworthy is He with our other types of anxiety? He sought us in the worst situation, and He will seek us in every other.

Yes, the sin of Adam and Eve has been passed down to us. Yes, we've inherited their corrupted nature along with the fear of judgment and death. Yes, we feel the result of their sin and suffering in our lives. But God's answer for sin, death, and suffering—a stronger covering, a better tree, and a greater Adam—is where hope resides. As Christians, we no longer need to be anxious about our story ending in guilt and shame because we hope in the Second Adam. We are clothed in Jesus Christ. The Christ who was nailed to the tree. The Christ who is our new and final representative. The Christ who stepped into our world, saved it, and rose again. The Christ who sent His Spirit to walk with us every step of our journey. The Christ who leads us to our Father, where we find rest and peace. There is no safer place to be.

Take heart: In the terrors of the fallen night, our God ran toward us. He sought us out, bringing with Him every solution to put our nightmares to rest. He tells us to snuggle up and bring our terrors to Him. And He will continue to walk closely with His children until the day He brings us home. If you are not a Christian, this seeking and covering is available for you in Christ as well.[20] There is a home waiting for us at the end of our hope.

20. If you are not a Christian, the Bible says, "If you confess with your mouth, 'Jesus is Lord,' and believe in your heart that God raised him from the dead, you will be saved" (Rom. 10:9). Right where you are, you can ask God for forgiveness for your sins, a heart of repentance, and trust in Jesus as your Savior and covering.

CHAPTER 6

Kiss the Waves

Some years ago, I had the privilege of listening to Joni Eareckson Tada pray. If you are unfamiliar with Sister Joni, she has paraplegia due to a diving accident that happened when she was seventeen. She dove into a shallow area in the Chesapeake Bay which left her paralyzed from the neck down. She has also dealt with two breast cancer diagnoses and has experienced tremendous suffering. I will never forget what she asked God for while in prayer. She asked God to help her to breathe.

Joni's prayer stuck with me because it revealed her level of dependence. Up to that point, I had never asked that in prayer. Not because I didn't need God to help me breathe, but because the ease with which I've been able to breathe throughout my life left me without feeling any need to ask for help from the One who allows me to breathe. Every human being needs God to breathe; each breath we take is God's doing. He is orchestrating our lungs and everything else required to inhale and exhale—all the result of God's merciful power. As Christians, we know Christ holds everything together, including our bodies and minds,[1] but Sister Joni knows this at a deeper level than most. Some people question those suffering with ailments and assume that their faith is ineffectual. It was through her physical affliction that she learned to truly rely upon God in a way she may not have if her circumstance were different. She says, speaking of God, "He has

1. Colossians 1:17

chosen not to heal me, but to hold me. The more intense the pain, the closer His embrace."[2]

In no way am I experiencing what Sister Joni is, but dealing with anxiety has caused me to recall her prayer, and I have had to ask God for the ability to breathe because of the panic attacks I have repeatedly faced. My anxiety revealed what I otherwise would never have acknowledged, which is I need God's help to do anything. I need His help breathing, seeing, driving, standing, making dinner, tying my shoes, sleeping, and more. I need Him to help me put one foot in front of the other each day as I journey in faith rather than walking in the shame we can often feel from others because of our afflictions. Our afflictions remind us that we're frail and unable to do anything without our God. In our churches and culture, to be unable or incapable of doing things on our own can be deemed shameful. Something must be wrong with us (and our faith) if our physical body shows signs of weakness. This is why the disciples asked Jesus a question in John 9.

There was a man born blind sitting near the temple gate. Jesus notices this man and his condition. His disciples asked Jesus, "Rabbi, who sinned, this man or his parents, that he was born blind?"[3] The Jews thought that calamities or infirmities were always the result of sin. We often assume the same. Jesus clarified for them that this man's blindness was not the result of sin at all, not his own nor his parents. Jesus responded to this man's suffering: "This came about so that God's work might be displayed in him."[4] God's work would be visible through this man who was born blind. This precious man and his infirmity were a part of God's wise divine plan. You are probably familiar with the rest of the story. Jesus makes mud and spreads it on his eyes. He then tells him to go and wash his eyes in the pool of Siloam. The man obeys, and he miraculously receives his sight.

Once the man can see, he is brought before the Pharisees. There is a contrast between his response and that of the religious leaders. The

2. Joni Eareckson Tada, *A Place of Healing: Wrestling with the Mysteries of Suffering, Pain, and God's Sovereignty* (David C. Cook, 2019), 40.
3. John 9:2
4. John 9:3

blind man humbly submitted to Jesus, while the religious leaders who thought they could see refused to. The blind man was considered sinful because of his condition, and the religious leaders were assumed to be without sin because of their position.

Like this blind man, each of us possesses some sort of weakness. Anxiety may be part of your weakness, and like the blind man, it may not be due to any sin in your life. The disciples were ready to condemn this man and accuse him of bringing this upon himself. But Jesus corrected this assumption and told them that the man's infirmity was given to him for a greater purpose. What if ours is too?

His Ways Are Higher Than Ours

Isaiah 55:8–9 is a well-known passage. It says,

> "For my thoughts are not your thoughts,
> and your ways are not my ways."
> This is the LORD's declaration.
> "For as heaven is higher than earth,
> so my ways are higher than your ways,
> and my thoughts than your thoughts."

Often, when we are suffering, it is hard to see past it to the overarching purpose God must have for it. In this way, anxiety can make us self-centered. Sometimes, all we see is our infirmity. It consumes our bodies and minds when we lack the vision to think about anything else. We wonder if our suffering is the result of our sin. Asking God about our sins is never a bad thing because anxiety *could* be the result of sin. The problem is we often lack other categories. Jesus (and the apostles) told us that we would experience suffering while on earth,[5] yet it's as if His words don't resonate with us. So, we go beyond repentance and beat ourselves up over our suffering. But there is no need for this harshness. Often suffering isn't due to an idol or to some deep, hidden sin. Sometimes, suffering is simply a part of life we must walk

5. John 16:33; Romans 8:17; 1 Peter 4:12–13; 5:10

through to be made more like Christ. If we are trembling through a certain leg of the Christian journey and our fear is not due to sin, we must conclude the affliction is outside of our control. Sometimes we find ourselves trembling through a general result of the Fall.[6] Other times we find ourselves shuddering from an attack from Satan.[7] Still other times, our affliction is appointed by God in a direct way, and we're *called* to tremble just as Christ was.[8] In terms of where the affliction is coming from, sometimes we can tell and sometimes we can't. But one thing is for certain: In any of these scenarios, Christians can respond the same way—the way the blind man did.

Physical Weakness and the Glory of God

The blind man trusted Jesus's words and went to the pool. We don't know if the road to get to the pool was bumpy and windy or smooth and straight. How far away was this pool? What amount of faith was required to reach the pool and be healed once he set out to obey Jesus's instructions? Did he have help to get there? All we know is that he went. He had faith in Christ and later he had boldness as he testified about what God had done for him. This example is helpful for us because the man's blindness was not the result of sin (which doesn't mean he had never sinned, but just that this suffering was not because of that). The Pharisees thought they had no sin,[9] and yet their sins remained.[10] This shows that it's not so much about having the ability to have working eyes. The Pharisees had eyes, yet they could not see their spiritual need. Because they had no sense of their need, they were not dependent upon Christ like this blind man was. Sometimes, when our eyes do not work, it creates humility in us, convincing us that we need someone with supernatural vision for us to see. The all-seeing eyes of God. Ultimately, in his deepest affliction, this man walked by faith and not by sight. In

6. Romans 8:17-25; 2 Corinthians 4:16–17
7. Luke 13:16; Acts 10:38
8. 1 Peter 2:20–21; Philippians 1:29; Acts 9:15–16
9. John 9:34
10. John 9:41

whatever our affliction is, we too must walk by faith. We must possess a vision that goes beyond physical sight and the limits of our physical bodies. This is how God's work is displayed through us in our weaknesses. Affliction creates the humility needed to seek out God. If we think we can see, we will never trust God for sight.[11]

What's my point? Anxiety, and all the trembling that comes from it, can be a surprising catalyst for opening our eyes, for helping us see, for driving us to the right place for comfort. We have an opportunity to see our anxiety as a frailty or physical difficulty put in place to convince us of our deeper need for intimacy with Jesus. Looking at our anxiety this way offers us a new season of humility, vulnerability, and dependency. It can also help us better understand our union with Christ as we cling to the only one who can open our eyes and calm the rains and winds blowing around and within us. Once we acknowledge that, we can go to God for what we know we do not have within ourselves. This is how God uses anxiety to display His work in us. The truth is, we are all frail and needy. Those of us who have been pushed to the end of ourselves know it.

I don't know what you are anxious about, but from one sufferer to another, I can tell you this: One silver lining with anxiety is that it can change you. Anxiety can be used as a mechanism to help you recognize your need to depend upon God. Anxiety exposes our physical limitations and limited resources, causing us to turn to the One with unlimited, sufficient resources. Having this perspective changes our entire relationship with anxiety because we see it for what it can be, a helper thrusting us into the presence of our Father. Sometimes we have been made to tremble in our anxiety so that we might more deeply tremble before God as we enjoy a deeper fellowship with Him. This is why James 1:2–4 says,

> Consider it a great joy, my brothers and sisters, whenever you experience various trials because you know that the testing of your faith produces endurance.

11. John 9:39–41

> And let endurance have its full effect, so that you may be mature and complete, lacking nothing.

James is not encouraging a stoicism where we act as though we feel no pain. Nor are we to be masochists who take pleasure in our physical pain and humiliation. We can acknowledge the difficulty of our suffering, and because of what it is producing in us—endurance, we can joyfully boast in our exaltation.[12] James is saying that we must keep the end in view as we go through our trials because endurance leads to the crown of life.[13] He reminds us of the purpose of our trials—including our anxiety—to grow in maturity.

Every anxious moment is an opportunity to grow in maturity. I don't mean plastering on a smile and pretending to be fine. I mean running toward Christ in your agony, allowing His truth to wash over you so that you're reminded of God's promises for you. We can trust God has a plan for each moment of weakness, each encounter with fear, and each wave of anxiety. These are opportunities for us to throw ourselves on the mercy of God and ask Him for what we need. Or, as the quote attributed to Spurgeon puts it: "I have learned to kiss the wave that throws me up against the Rock of Ages."[14] As we rely upon God the Rock and not ourselves, we find His joy as we endure, putting to death self-reliance and identifying as one who is united with Christ in suffering.[15] *Help us kiss these waves, Lord. Remind us of the excellent purpose You are working in us through our suffering.*

Neediness, Weakness, and Reckoning with Capacity

Have you ever been in the place where your capacity suddenly drops and you're wondering why all your stamina and energy has

12. James 1:9
13. James 1:12
14. There is no evidence Spurgeon said this. The closest quote is found in his 1874 sermon "Sin and Grace": "The wave of temptation may even wash you higher up upon the Rock of ages, so that you cling to it with a firmer grip than you have ever done before, and so again where sin abounds, grace will much more abound."
15. Philippians 3:10–11

petered out like a phone bought four years ago? You want to keep going at the pace you are used to, but your body says, "No!" It feels like failure in a way nothing else does. You feel like you're drowning in "shoulds"—I *should* be able to make the extracurricular events, I *should* be able to homeschool, I *should* be able to meal prep and serve at church and minister to neighbors. I *should* be able to *drive*, for crying out loud!

That was the season I was in when it became clear that some things needed to change in terms of my commitments and my schedule. It's hard to reckon with the truth in those moments. I had to realize that this particular season was going to be different than the others when it came to my capacity. I wrestled with that until I finally surrendered. Of course, it took time to get there. Anxiety had started to make me feel like a startled child: needy, exposed, susceptible, sensitive, jumpy. Psychologists call this hypervigilance. This trembling made me feel vulnerable and helpless. I was used to being the wife-mom-homeschooling-driver-discipler-minister-poet-Bible teacher who cared for everyone else. Yet, there I was, suddenly unable to care for myself. My body was unable to do that which my mind told it to, and each bodily symptom triggered additional catastrophic thoughts.

Two years into this battle with anxiety, as my capacity shrank along with my confidence, my husband decided to leave pastoral ministry. In part because he wanted to care for me. My inability to do the things I did before meant that he needed to prioritize his first ministry: our family. This decision was a lot for me to process. I mean, we moved to plant a church and two years in, the ministry plans were changing. This new turn of events, and my part to play in it, advanced my anxiety. I ended up spiraling down deeper in my anxiety but also deeper in the shame that often accompanies it.

My mind and body finally forced me to clear away anything on my plate I could live without. This compelled me to acknowledge that while I am made in the image of God, I am not God. Neither am I the Hindu false god Shiva, portrayed with several hands, as though he is able to carry the load of a superhuman. I cleared my schedule of all speaking engagements. I pushed away the dreams of my accelerated online class schedule. I put our children in school. I stripped down from things I enjoyed but no longer had the capacity for. This deep sea of cares was my new world, and the only way to swim through it was to surrender my own strength and let God keep me afloat.

There Is Only One Who Is Strong

"What *about* God allowed you to stay afloat?" you may wonder. Many things, but for the purposes of this chapter, I'll center on three of His attributes that anxiety forced me to rely upon in deeper ways than ever before. Despite my fears (and yours), I learned on a whole new level that our unchangeable, all-powerful, all-knowing God never trembles. Considering the central attributes of God when I was (and when you are) afraid reminded me that we serve an in-control God, who is omnipotent, omniscient, and filled with omnibenevolence. These attributes may be familiar to you on a shallow level, but I pray they be a buoy providing direction amid the chaotic sea.

God's Omnipotence

Omnipotence means God is "all-powerful." He is distinct from creation as the sovereign ruler with unlimited power consistent with His nature.[16] As the Creator of everything, He has complete power over all He has made. We see God displaying His unlimited power not only in creating[17] but in upholding creation by the word of His power.[18] The elements of nature are submissive to Him.[19] He has complete power over life and death,[20] and they submit to Him.[21] The laws of nature bend when He chooses to move miraculously, like we see with the virgin birth,[22] or the miraculous signs of restoring bodies riddled with

16. Ephesians 1:11
17. Genesis 2:1; John 1:3; Psalm 148:3–5; Hebrews 11:3
18. Colossians 1:17; Hebrews 1:3
19. Matthew 8:27; John 6:15–21
20. Deuteronomy 32:39; 1 Samuel 2:6
21. Acts 17:25; John 5:21; John 11:44
22. Isaiah 7:14

disease.[23] He has authority over demonic powers[24] and will destroy the devil's works.[25] God's authority spans all things visible and invisible. All things are under His rule.

Knowing that God is omnipotent should help us in two ways: 1) to strengthen our faith in His abilities now, and 2) to help us hope in His divine justice later. Jeremiah 32:17 says, "Oh, Lord God! You yourself made the heavens and earth by your great power and with your outstretched arm. Nothing is too difficult for you!" Since God is above all things, we can trust Him. Our circumstances are not out of His control. Each detail that has us trembling is under His control and will be used as a part of His divine purpose in our lives. If He wants to bring our anxiousness to a halt, He certainly can. If He wants us to suffer, He has promised as the omnipotent One to exert His power as our protector-guide on this journey. It's freeing to know that God is all-powerful, and anxiety is not.

Second, we can trust the divine justice of our omnipotent King. It can be discouraging when we suffer because of circumstances that are out of our control or even within our control. Scripture tells us that suffering, for righteousness' sake, means that we can entrust ourselves to Him who judges righteously.[26] God has promised to restore His children by rewarding them for their perseverance.[27] When the final judgment comes, we know that we can confidently rest in the perfect judgment of God, as we do not boast in our righteousness but entirely hide ourselves in the righteousness of Christ.

God's Omniscience

Not only is God omnipotent, but He is also omniscient. *Omniscience* means that God is "all-knowing" and nothing can surprise Him about the past, present, or future. Our Eternal, Divine God

23. Matthew 9:27–31
24. Matthew 8:28–29, 32; Colossians 2:15
25. 1 John 3:8; Revelation 20:10
26. 1 Peter 2:23
27. Romans 2:6–7

knows everything simultaneously. He never grows in understanding but knows the beginning and the end just the same. He knows all things,[28] and there is no limit to His wisdom.[29]

> Oh, the depth of the riches
> and the wisdom and the knowledge of God!
> How unsearchable his judgments
> and untraceable his ways!
> For who has known the mind of the Lord?
> Or who has been his counselor?
> And who has ever given to God,
> that he should be repaid?
> For from him and through him
> and to him are all things.
> To him be the glory forever. Amen.[30]

God's intelligence cannot be held or contained because there is no end to its depth. He has no counselor that He looks to for advice.[31] He owes nothing to anyone because He is the sole source of His knowledge. He knows every detail of our lives—our actions,[32] our hearts,[33] and even our anxious thoughts.[34] While in the womb,[35] he counts every hair on our head and knows when a sparrow falls.[36] David said, "You observe my travels and my rest; you know all my ways."[37] Since God is all-knowing, He grasps the exhaustive details of our anxiety. He knows the full measure of our affliction. Anxious symptoms keep the mind tottering when the heart is beating, pounding, and irregular, and the Lord is not unaware. Not only is He privy to the full scope of

28. 1 John 3:18–20
29. Psalm 17:5
30. Romans 11:33–36
31. Job 36:22–23; Isaiah 40:13–14
32. Psalm 139:2
33. 1 Kings 8:39
34. Psalm 139:24
35. Psalm 139:15–17
36. Luke 12:7
37. Psalm 139:3

our pain, but He is also compassionate regarding us and the suffering we are going through.[38]

God's Omnibenevolence

God's *omnibenevolence* means that He is "all good." Goodness is His nature, and it is reserved for Him alone.[39] Psalm 145:9 says, "The LORD is good to everyone; his compassion rests on all he has made." God deals with His creation with love, goodness, and divine pity. He causes His sun to rise on the evil and the good and sends rain on the righteous and the unrighteous.[40] He is willing to bless any who will accept His good and perfect gifts.[41]

Again, I'd be willing to wager you already know these attributes of God. But I share them with you again because we anxious people can be so overwhelmed by our anxieties that these truths are easy to forget. Also, because all of these attributes wrapped up together means something crucial: God is unafraid, which means He is the ideal person to run to when you are afraid. There's nothing in this universe that can threaten Him. He has no limits in His ability to help. He's the perfect person to trust in your anxiety journey because He will never be busy dealing with His own.

This is who these anxious waves are thrusting you upon: the One who has all the power and who loves you dearly. If you need the power to press through your journey, He is all-powerful. If you need the reminder that wrongs will be set right, He is all-just. If you need the wisdom to handle each wave of anxiety in a godly way, He is all-wise. If you need someone to understand the full range of the anxiety you feel today—the highs and the lows—He is all-knowing. If you need someone kind on the weak days and a reminder that this journey will not turn out for your harm, He is all-good.

---

38. Psalm 56:8; Isaiah 30:18
39. Mark 10:18; Matthew 19:17
40. Matthew 5:45
41. James 1:17

You will go through bouts of fear. But your God is unafraid. He is higher than any mountain in your life. Unafraid of your needs. Unafraid of your natural fears. Unafraid of your worst fears. Unafraid of your sinful fears. He's worth trusting in this journey. He has sufficient resources. His skill set brings peace to your division and calm to your quivering body. If the anxiety never vanishes, we still praise Him. If we never slept well again, continued with stomach issues, always felt faint, couldn't breathe properly, remained sensitive to light, couldn't drive beyond an hour, or woke up each night with deer or something else on the brain, we would still have a sovereign God by our side.

Before we go anywhere, we must start there by embracing the waves in our life. Why? Because it throws us upon our Rock of Ages. God is the Rock that will not crumble. God is the Rock that is our steady, immovable, unshakable fortress. He alone is our rock and our salvation, our stronghold. Because He is in control of every wave in the ultimate sense, we will never be shaken.[42]

I want you to map out some time over the next few days to revisit God's character and promises. Find a quiet place to look back at this chapter and meditate on our Rock of Ages who is omnipotent, omniscient, and omnibenevolent.

42. Psalm 62:2

CHAPTER 7

More Than a Soul

Humans are like a braid intricately woven of spirit, soul, *and* body. The Bible uses various terms to describe the immaterial parts of our humanity: heart, soul, spirit, mind, and so on. It also uses various terms to describe the material part of us: body, flesh, members, and so on. When we look backward at the start of our human story, Scripture reveals that when God created us "The LORD God formed man *of* the dust of the ground, and breathed into his nostrils the breath of life; and man became a living soul."[1] When we look to the end of our human story, Scripture reveals that redeemed humanity will not be a disembodied spirit but a whole person in the resurrection, with material and immaterial parts woven together.

So, what does this have to do with anxiety? The fact that you exist as both a material *and* immaterial being means that any help you receive in relation to your anxiety should include the entirety of your being, both physical and spiritual components. If you're anything like me, perhaps that comes as a surprise to you. I always thought anxiety—or any other struggle in life—was predominately handled in the spiritual realm. Up until the last few years of my life, all the advice I knew of, all the typical responses I received, all the counsel I had explored—they were all only spiritual. I had no idea part of anxiety was physical, until I experienced it myself. Our whole life and walk with God should include the body and not just the soul. I thought that because of the work of Christ done in His body, that I should never have any physical or psychological struggles in mine. And I was not

1. Genesis 2:7 KJV

alone. As I looked around at other believers, I realized that so often, we ignore our mental health and only emphasize our spiritual sanctification. I saw that, unfortunately, the church often takes on Platonic anthropology, segregating and downplaying our physical body like modern Gnostics. Maybe you grew up in conditions that had the value placed on the other side of the spectrum. Maybe everything in your life revolves around solving problems either physically or logistically, and your soul-care has been neglected. Either way, the Bible has good news for you: God isn't interested in only ministering to one part of you during your anxiety journey. He wants to minister to *every* part of your humanity. Scriptures teach that God created the body and spirit and called them both good.

The Already and Not Yet

We should listen to God as He walks us through how to experience holistic ministry. This means we should make room for our complete selves—the material and the immaterial. God tells us expressly that in between the beginning and the end, God is sanctifying our inner and outer self thoroughly. "Now may the God of peace himself sanctify you completely. And may your whole spirit, soul, and body be kept sound and blameless at the coming of our Lord Jesus Christ."[2] Theologians call this "meantime" something hopeful: the already and not yet. We belong to God. We've *already* been "made us alive together with Christ."[3] Our position in Christ is set to the point that the apostle Paul talks about our salvation in the past tense: He "raised us up with him and seated us with him in the heavenly places in Christ Jesus."[4] In other words, from our point of view, our future position in eternity has *not yet* come to pass, but from God's point of view, it's so certain that He considers it as good as done. We can take hope in this.

On the days when we feel like we've been painted by Picasso—when we feel like we are a disjointed disruption of several hues left

2. 1 Thessalonians 5:23
3. Ephesians 2:5 ESV
4. Ephesians 2:6

aloof—we remember that God made the spirit and the body, and He says they are good. We also can use spiritual, emotional, physical, and mental helps. When our spirit is low, our mental health is suffering, our body is overwhelmed, or our spirit is discouraged, He offers us certain helps and tools to minister to us. As He works to sanctify our entire self, He is not merely ministering to our spirit, but He is ministering to our bodies too. What kinds of help does He give?

Spiritual Helps: God's Word, God's Spirit, and God's Ear

God's Word

The first way God helps us is through His Word. Over and against the patterns and ideas that stem from this world, "All Scripture is inspired by God and is profitable for teaching, for rebuking, for correcting, for training in righteousness."[5] As we learn God's Word and internalize it, we find that it has great power to renew and transform the way we move through life.[6] God's Word encourages us and helps us not only understand the world but also helps us learn how to walk in it wisely. God's Holy Word is not only for our spirit but can separate between our inner and outer parts of spirit, soul and body, judging us completely as a whole being.

> For the word of God is living and effective and sharper than any double-edged sword, penetrating as far as the separation of soul and spirit, joints and marrow. It is able to judge the thoughts and intentions of the heart.[7]

In other words, the Word of God has the power to minister to us in a variety of ways, through conviction, but it also comes through

5. 2 Timothy 3:16
6. Romans 12:2
7. Hebrews 4:12

encouragement and consolation during the darkest nights of the body and soul.

God's Spirit

The second way God helps us spiritually is through His Spirit. God's mercy and grace are lavished upon us, saving our spirit, soul, and body from judgment. Once we have received Christ, we are filled with God's Spirit. Through the Holy Spirit, we can put to death the misdeeds of the body, not succumbing to its desires.[8] We can live out our spiritual gifts, we can bear godly fruit, we can overcome the mindset of the flesh, and we can combat the lies of the enemy which wage war in our anxious minds.

God's Ear

The power of prayer is a third way God helps us spiritually, since Scripture says that His ear listens to the cries of His people.[9] We must pray because we are helpless apart from God. We must pray because through it we know and enjoy God. We must pray because it is the means by which God brings change in us and, if He wills, also in our circumstances. Since a prayer is oftentimes a request, God may or may not respond with a yes. Remember Jesus in the garden of Gethsemane prayed three times for the Father to take the cross away and the answer was consistently "no."[10] Jesus's response was, "Not my will, but yours, be done." A consistent prayer life through faith in the Spirit does not mean automatic removal of suffering; it does mean grace in the trial to conform us to our Christlike identity. Prayer is a way to lay our requests before our God because we have a Father who loves to listen.

---

8. Romans 6:12
9. Psalm 34:15
10. Matthew 26:44–46

Using God's Word to Speak Truth to Yourself

Not only do we have the privilege of talking to God, but we must talk to ourselves. This is another way to fight to have an influence in what direction our thoughts go. If they are going in a direction that does not serve us or the Lord, we seek to take those thoughts captive through prayer like the sons of Korah who spoke to their soul.

> Why, my soul, are you so dejected?
> Why are you in such turmoil?
> Put your hope in God, for I will still praise him,
> my Savior and my God.[11]

Sometimes that can look like reminding yourself of the Scriptures. It can also look like reminding yourself of what is true. Let me give you an example. Often during my time at church, I would feel faint and like I might have a panic attack. I would feel this especially when it was time to stand and sing. As I would try to stand up while having these physical symptoms, the thought would come to me, *What if I faint?* I would then be flooded with a slew of mental comments and questions like, *Oh no, that would be awful! If I fainted, then they would have to call the ambulance . . . there would be a huge scene which would take the focus off of the service . . . and it would be a major distraction . . .* The thoughts of what could happen if I succumb to my symptoms would spiral me into a wild frenzy of endless possibilities. I figured I had to carry these thoughts myself because I didn't want anyone to be burdened by them like I was. It felt like I was carrying 300 pound weights on my mind. Weights that were too heavy for me to uphold. Weights that wouldn't allow me to worship because I was so distracted. These thoughts would overtake me Sunday after Sunday, all springing from my physical symptoms.

One Sunday, when the thoughts started, I had a moment of clarity I hadn't had before, and God allowed me to respond to myself, using

11. Psalm 42:11

my own mental agency. I posed a question to myself: *What is the worst that could happen?*

Really? What could happen? I then began to think about it . . . *If I were to faint right here at church . . . It would be embarrassing . . . but I would be surrounded by a group of people who know me, love me, and would want to care for me. They may call the ambulance, and that is okay. An ambulance coming to church would not disrupt their relationship with God.* Something I realized through counseling was that because of my upbringing, I always felt pressure to not make a fuss or be a burden to others. Because of this, the idea that I would be needy and cause someone inconvenience was a huge problem that made me anxious. It went against everything I was subliminally trained in and further activated my *anxiety*! It took many Sundays, but I eventually convinced myself that if an ambulance was needed then it was worth having, since God says I'm worth caring for. Things would keep going. All would be okay. And I wouldn't die because I was having a panic attack, not a heart attack. I also realized my church family would pray for me and follow up to make sure I was okay. I mean, even if I did die, I'd be with the Lord and eventually be raised to new life in the resurrection, where I'd see them all again anyway. Seeing things from this perspective produced a shift for me. It didn't take away all my physical symptoms, but it helped me realize that some of what was behind my angst, and even made it worse, was this insecurity of feeling safe or cared for and the lie that I would be an inconvenience.

Asking these questions in other areas began to set me free from the typical and chaotic train of thought I was previously conditioned to ride. I began to ask myself questions in other anxious scenarios, especially when driving. *What if another deer comes along and I hit it? I know it's rare, but what is the worst that could happen? Because it very well could happen again. So, what's the worst? I could die. I could have another panic attack. I could be physically injured.* Then I had this comforting thought: *If these fears came true, and my entire world was shaken or taken, there is one thing I would have. I would still have God.* God would never abandon me in the midst of these tragedies or trials. He would not even abandon me in death. His presence and comfort would keep me regardless of the result. If I have another attack, He is there. If I die, I will be present with Him. If I were physically harmed, I can find safety in His gaze.[12]

It turns out this very process of asking, "Oh yeah, and what if? What if the worst thing you can imagine actually happens?" is what some counselors use to help their clients manage anxiety in cognitive-behavioral therapy. They use this technique not so that their clients stay in a state of fear but to pull back the layers of the fear. I was led to do this naturally but there is science to support this kind of thought process helping to reduce anxiety. Seeing that the worst thing we fear might not be as bad as we think helps us have agency to address it; it reduces the power that fear has over us.

Seizing our anxious thoughts and holding them up to what God actually says about us—that we're loved, that we're safe in Him, that He is with us no matter the outcome—takes time and repeated effort, but it's a practice that really does bring good news to our worst-case scenarios.

Emotional Helps: Jesus Is Our Counselor, Intercessor, and Friend

Along with spiritual help, God offers us emotional help. And He does so in three ways. Our first kind of emotional help is divine comfort. In John 14:16 Jesus said, "I will ask the Father, and he will give you another Counselor [or Comforter] to be with you forever." Jesus is the Counselor and the Holy Spirit would be the other Counselor. One way Jesus comforts us is through being in solidarity with us, by becoming human like us. His incarnational ministry looks like choosing to identify with humanity for the sake of redeeming us, but also for the sake of relationship with us. The writer of Hebrews says:

> For we do not have a high priest who is unable to sympathize with our weaknesses, but one who has been ***tempted in every way as we are,*** yet without sin. Therefore, let us approach the throne of grace

12. Psalm 139:1–18

> with boldness, so that we may receive mercy and find grace to help us in time of need.[13]

You don't have to wonder if God knows what it's like to be you, or if the Lord "gets it" when you've had a hard day. The writer of Hebrews makes it clear that Jesus not only gets it, He gets it *in every way*. Christ feels your pain and knows your struggles because He's been there too, and He understands what it means to be human in every possible respect, except sin. "He can deal gently with the ignorant and wayward, since *he himself* is beset with weakness."[14] Your Savior knows what it is to have infirmity, to be tired, thirsty, angry, agonizing, troubled, and weak. He stands with you in your pain, as one who truly understands.

Along with Jesus's solidarity as our Counselor, we can rest in the emotional support of Jesus's intercession. Again, the book of Hebrews helps us:

> Therefore, [Jesus] is able to save completely those who come to God through him, since he always lives to intercede for them.[15]

Ever wonder what Jesus is doing all day now that He's risen and ascended, sitting at the right hand of the Father? The answer is this: He's praying for you. He lives, day and night, to intercede for His people. On the days you don't know what to pray for yourself, your heavenly Priest and Intercessor is already interceding on your behalf. When you notice you are engaging in sinful fear, He goes to war on your behalf. On top of that, He is able to do this for you forever. Why? Because His mediating ability to connect you to the Father is a ministry that will never end. He will live forever in His resurrected state, which means His mediating power will always work on your behalf, from now till kingdom come, and beyond. You are united to Him

13. Hebrews 4:15–16, emphasis added
14. Hebrews 5:2 ESV
15. Hebrews 7:25

today, tomorrow, and forever, and He will never stop mediating for you and interceding for you.

Not only does Jesus relate to us in solidarity and intercession, but He also draws us into loving friendship. In John 15:13–15 Jesus says this to the disciples, "No one has greater love than this: to lay down his life for his friends. You are my friends if you do what I command you. I do not call you servants anymore, because a servant doesn't know what his master is doing. I have called you friends, because I have made known to you everything I have heard from my Father." Jesus displayed the greatest type of love through His death. We show that we belong to God through loving Him back and doing what He commands us. On the hard days you feel like you don't have a good friend available, the truth is this: Yes, you do. Jesus is not distant emotionally speaking. He not only gets you and intercedes for you, but He's a true friend, here any time you need Him.

Communal Helps

Sometimes God brings the manna Himself, but other times He wants a human to get their hands in the dirt and plant some wheat so that the baker down the street can take the crop and make bread for the community. Said another way, sometimes the help comes directly from God, but other times, it comes from people made in His image. If you are facing some sort of spiritual or emotional need (or physical need, which we'll get to in a moment), it's always wise to ask God for help—but also ask for help from people too. One of the greatest ways God tends to us as we tremble under the weight of life is to send others to stand beside us, lift up our arms, and bear the weight with us. So, lean into the communal help offered by your friendships, fellow church members, family members, counselors, and neighbors. What emotional or physical needs do you have? Who could you ask for help? Or, if you're in a season where you could be the helper, who in your life right now needs you to help them in an emotional, physical, or practical sense? It may mean helping them move, listening to their struggles, playing with their kids for a few hours at the playground, or making a meal. There are many ways to help someone in need and ask for help when you are in need.

Talk to a Counselor

A licensed counselor can help you process your past, identify any negative thought-patterns that might be getting in your way, offer you practical strategies for navigating anxiety, and give you many more valuable tools. The Bible says there is wisdom to be gleaned from an abundance of good counselors.[16] Most of us don't have even one good one. But we'd do well to get one, because anxiety can be hard to navigate alone. Anxiety is like an iceberg, floating, frozen, and frightful in size. We are aware of the visible parts, the obvious symptoms, but often there is much more we cannot see. Finding a counselor can be a great help toward addressing the part that is underneath the surface.

In my own anxiety journey, I eventually realized I needed some help sorting through the fears I was experiencing. After all, when your capacity is lower than ever and your anxiety is higher than ever, you're out of your depth and you need the ministry of a guide through the floodwaters. I asked a friend if they would recommend a counselor. We had an initial evaluation and began meeting every other week. My first counselor was a Christian therapist. She asked questions about both my family of origin and my nuclear family. She looked at my symptoms and how they might be connected. I sat skeptical of her and how she was making connections that appeared to be shifting from me and my accident to my upbringing. I met with her for about four months. Then, after my husband left the pastorate, I found Mrs. Stately. She was also a Christian therapist. She has been a pastor's wife for over forty years and a counselor for over twenty-five. We connected right away during our first meeting. She encouraged me, like an experienced captain familiar with navigating a boat in this ocean, suggesting that the waves would not always be this overpowering. Yes, life would bring with it burdens and cares, but this level-10, acute post-traumatic stress didn't usually last forever at the high range it was blasting now. For the

16. Proverbs 11:14

first time I was able to see slightly beyond the showers. With her words, a ray of sunshine peeked through.

I was vulnerable with her about all the ways I hated being made vulnerable because of my anxiety. We talked about the event itself, about driving, about the panic attacks and other symptoms. She asked me about my upbringing, and I began to see how my childhood *did* connect to my anxiety. Not for the purpose of blame, but to address that which had been unaddressed for too long. She counseled me both spiritually and physically—from scriptural encouragement, to eye-motion exercises designed to desensitize traumatic memories, to breathing techniques, to encouraging me to blast gospel music while driving, to reminding me to cry out to God, and to pay attention to my self-talk. She would close each of our meetings with prayer. I felt supported for the first time, like I had someone in my corner who understood my stage of life and cares and would hold my hand to help me through this.

Eventually, I was able to drive for about fifteen minutes. Then twenty. Then thirty. Then I could finally drive my children to school! For the next three years, I could drive for an hour, but not a minute more. I then could make the three-hour drive to DC with a friend in the car. Now I am able to drive by myself without any limits or fears impacting me. That's what my struggle with anxiety has been like in certain seasons: not one and done, but bit-by-bit over time, thanks to good counselors and a very good God.

Help Makes You Remember

One benefit of having a good counselor is that they help you put the pieces of your own story together, connecting dots and helping you see threads that have been running throughout your life without your notice. Author and therapist Hilary Jacobs Hendel says anxiety along with shame and guilt are an inhibitor emotion used to block core emotions. When we are taught to hide our core emotions (fear, anger, sadness, disgust, joy, excitement) or if, during our childhood, we were punished for expressing them, we learn to cope through anxiety and find other ways to put up defenses. These defenses can manifest in several ways like sarcasm, smiling, spacing out, tiredness, procrastination, perfectionism, etc.[17] When I finally got help, I realized that while intellectually anxiety felt new to my mind, experientially it was not new to my body. Things began to make more sense.

I told you after the car accident, I had my first panic attack. During a journaling session, I later remembered that I had one years earlier. When I was around eighteen years old, I took myself to the hospital because I felt like I couldn't breathe. It was during a very stressful time in life. I was overwhelmed. Again, the doctors never said what it was. I followed up with a primary care doctor. This is the only time in my life I had high blood pressure. I remember him asking me, "What's going on in your life right now?" I was so taken aback, that I froze and said, "Nothing, really." I didn't understand that what this doctor was doing—connecting what was happening physically in my body to events and stressors in my life—was important to unlocking the source of the symptoms I was experiencing.

Even before that, when I was thirteen, I lost my brother to Sudden Infant Death Syndrome (SIDS). It happened while my mother was in jail. My seventeen-year-old sister and I were thrust into the responsibility of caring for ourselves and our infant brother that month. He was two months old. I woke up around 5:30–6:00 a.m. and got my brother fed, burped, changed, and laid him back down in the middle of my mother's bed. Back then, we were told to lay a baby down on their stomach. I did that. Then I headed to the bus stop to catch my school bus. Of course, when I got the call later that day, I couldn't believe my ears that my baby brother was gone. Though I did everything I had been told to do with a baby that age, I blamed myself since I was the last person to lay him down.

For the first few years on the anniversary of his death, I could smell the scent that was in the morgue, and I remember running out of class in tears. I felt like I couldn't breathe and was on the verge of vomiting. While I remember a classmate running out to comfort me, I never

17. Hilary Jacobs Hendel, *It's Not Always Depression: Working the Change Triangle to Listen to the Body, Discover Core Emotions, and Connect to Your Authentic Self* (Random House, 2018), "Kindle," 16–20.

talked to a counselor. No one ever asked what I needed. I couldn't talk about or express the sadness I felt. So, I buried the emotion and held on to a lingering grief and guilt. Our family never talked about it. When I tried, I was met with punishment in the form of disapproval by a single mother trying to survive—trying to somehow grieve her own son and personal choices with no time or resources to process the pain. Certainly, she couldn't help me process my pain. Running out of class in tears overwhelmed by grief was that emotion seeping out into an anxiety attack mingled with shame and guilt. Fast-forward, I recall how terrified I was when I had my first child. I held my baby boy in my arms and wondered if God would allow him to live past two months. Would God take him away like He did my brother? Do you see the unaddressed emotional dots and how they connect?

When we experience traumatic events and we just tuck them away and keep living, eventually our body and/or mind says, "No more!" *Anxiety is the body speaking.* I have since worked through my brother's death and learned more details about the situation and that it wasn't my fault. I didn't learn about this until I talked about my brother's death with my family twelve years later, and I didn't get counseling for it until my car accident—over twenty years later. Before my accident, I never would've considered myself anxious, but now I look back and see it was always there. There were other hints too, like how I bit my nails from three years old until I was in high school. I still sometimes nibble on the skin around my nail bed. Or how I learned at home and through theater classes how to hide my anxiety behind masking tactics so that "the show could go on." Anxiety was right under my nose, but I was either unaware or in denial of the scent. Thank the Lord for the mental, and emotional, help God sends us in counselors who know how to awaken our sense of smell.

Medicine and Providence

An older woman I connected with who is also a ministry wife shared that she was on a low dose of anti-anxiety medicine and probably would be for the rest of her life. It has been a great help to her. I appreciate how she said this matter-of-factly and without any hovering shame. She didn't connect medicine to character at all. This helped me as I tried medicine out for the first time. Doctors agree that medicine is not an exact science. Sometimes they know why a given medicine works and sometimes only that it does seem to work. Even then, it may work for some and not others. This is why this is a conversation that is best had with your doctor and those who love you.[18] My primary care physician would often ask me at the end of each appointment if I wanted to try an antidepressant. I would respond, "No thanks. I don't feel depressed, so I am not sure why an antidepressant would be necessary." He didn't specify that most anti-depressant medications (SSRIs) are also used to treat anxiety. After refusing, I tried a prescription medication and concluded that due to the side effects, it wasn't the best fit for me. I found a supplement that is a stress-support blend of herbs and vitamins that has helped me greatly. If you are cleared by your doctor to take medications or supplements, just know that it is not a blemish on your character, nor will there be marks against your salvation. Paul was not at all slighting Timothy's spiritual life when he encouraged him to take a remedy for his stomach issues and frequent sickness.[19] The medicine may have helped Timothy serve more effectively. For many, medicine or incorporating supplements for a designated time can be a Godsend and is the difference between being able to have the capacity to think clear thoughts and serve their families or communities well, or not. When it comes to our physical ailments or mental health, God could provide miraculous healing by taking away all anxieties in a moment. But He often helps us by way of doctors to prescribe medicine and wise counselors to offer therapy too.

18. If your doctor does suggest you consider medication, I recommend you share that with a few trusted loved ones since one of the potential side effects of many anti-anxiety or anti-depression medications is suicidal despair. So, make sure that you and those around you can love you well and be there to support you if those thoughts creep in.
19. 1 Timothy 5:23

A word on healing is in order. At times, God heals in stages[20] or uses image-bearers to assist us in the process.[21] He could have us get water from a rock[22] or tell someone to give us a drink.[23] God uses different kinds of approaches, depending upon His plan. We don't have to pit Jesus miraculously feeding the 5,000 men, women, and children bread and fish against the widow used to make bread for Elijah with a little oil and flour, against God giving manna from heaven. Nor should we pit a Christian therapist (or for that matter a secular therapist endowed with common grace)[24] seeking to care for an anxiety-stricken counselee against a pastor who faithfully preaches and applies God's Word each week. They don't have to go against one another; both can be used in discipleship. In Tim Keller's book *Every Good Endeavor*, he argues against the secular-sacred divide as he quotes Martin Luther who views the divide regarding professions as an invention because "all Christians are truly of the spiritual estate, and there is no difference among them except that of office."[25]

Physical Helps: Improve Basic Rhythms and Limit the Things That Disrupt Them

One way we receive physical help is to simply lean into the way God designed humans. We are limited creatures, with natural thresholds for how much we can handle. We must eat, drink, sleep, breathe, live, rest, and worship to experience human flourishing and abundant life. God helps us by giving us an internal clock when it's time to rest, hunger pangs when it's time to eat, and thirst when it's time to drink. But we must take Him up on that help and act on it. We still must

20. Mark 8:24–26
21. 1 Kings 17:13–14
22. Exodus 17:6
23. Mark 9:41
24. John Murray defines common grace as "every favour of whatever kind or degree, falling short of salvation, which this undeserving and sin-cursed world enjoys at the hand of God" ("Common Grace," in *Collected Writings of John Murray*, Volume II, Philadelphia, PA, 1977, 96).
25. Tim Keller, *Every Good Endeavor: Connecting Your Work to God's Work* (Penguin, 2012), 58.

responsibly nurture ourselves and make wise choices. If we fight this design—for example, if we stay up late as a rule, never giving the body the Sabbath it needs—we will end up in a physical crisis. If you're struggling physically, start with this question: Have you been neglecting any of these basic rhythms (eating, drinking, sleeping, resting, and worship)? Why? Sometimes we *are* living according to God's design, and we still get sick or find ourselves struggling with a brain-related issue (or get into an accident, like I did). Other times our sickness is due to a disruption in the healthy rhythms meant to help us thrive.

Scripture does not treat Christians as disembodied souls when Paul writes to the Corinthians,

> Don't you know that your body is a temple of the Holy Spirit who is in you, whom you have from God? You are not your own, for you were bought at a price. So glorify God with your body.[26]

Notice Paul doesn't just give them spiritual answers for their problems. He says their main source of help is going to come from doing something specific with their *bodies*. In their day, the specific task they were called to was to stop joining their physical body with prostitutes. This practice harmed their own body and displeased God. In our day, it would do us well to ask: What might I be doing with my body that harms it and displeases God? What could I start doing with my body that might help heal the problem I'm facing right now?

Stimulants and Social Media

For me, one of the answers to that last question was to cut off stimulants. These do not necessarily displease God each time they are used, but they were not helping my anxiety. I'm a black tea drinker. One day, after I shared my anxiety struggles with a friend, she brought up not only how much tea I was drinking but how long I would steep the bag because I like my black tea strong. I had never noticed it, but

26. 1 Corinthians 6:19–20; see Romans 8:10–13, 22–25

she did. I knew that this was probably impacting my anxiety, as caffeine is a stimulant that increases blood pressure and heart rate, so I decided to come off it for a couple years. I found it did improve how I felt! I also scaled back my sugar intake with good effects.

Tea and sugar aren't the only stimulants I've had to scale back on from time to time. Another stimulant we overindulge in but do not measure by the teaspoon is social media. With social media at our fingertips, we know that the risks outweigh the benefits. We have more followers than any other time in our life and are lonelier than ever before. Teens especially are at risk. If a teen spends more than three hours a day on social media, they are twice as likely to have symptoms of depression and/or anxiety.[27] And with the current algorithms, if a teen (or adult) researches a topic like depression, self-harm, or anxiety, they will then be fed more content related to those topics. Before they know it, they can be surrounded by content creators who are all struggling with depression, self-harm, and/or anxiety.[28] While a sense of feeling understood or healthy recommendations might be benefits, there is also risk in exposure to more rumination or otherwise unhealthy or unhelpful content. We are in a social experiment and we don't know all the effects of thrusting ourselves into the apps. But the bottom line is social media is producing changes at societal, group, family, and individual levels, and while the long-term outcomes are unknown, the evidence for mental health isn't looking good. I have had to listen when my only audience is the Almighty; when He is telling me to lower my social media engagement and I obey, I find it helps my anxiety calm.

I'm happy to say that over the past year or so I have begun to enjoy a cup of tea or coffee again. There are moments when I find myself feeling anxious and I do have to think about how much caffeine I've

---

27. Kira E. Riehm, Kenneth A. Feder, Kayla N. Tormohlen, et al. "Associations Between Time Spent Using Social Media and Internalizing and Externalizing Problems Among US Youth," *JAMA Psychiatry* 76, no. 12 (2019):1266–1273, doi:10.1001/jamapsychiatry.2019.2325.

28. Kathy Katella, "How Social Media Affects Your Teen's Mental Health: A Parent's Guide," Yale Medicine, June 17, 2024, https://www.yalemedicine.org/news/social-media-teen-mental-health-a-parents-guide.

had. Often, I can link how I feel to how many cups of tea I've had that morning and how much sugar is in front of me. But the larger point is that there are things that sometimes hurt our anxious bodies—things God is asking us to unjoin from our bodies (or unglue from our eyes) for a season. For me, that was caffeine, sugar, and social media. What might it be for you?

A final source of physical help is dance. Yes. I said dance! When was the last time you did the electric slide, or salsa'd your way to calm? A recent study showed that dancing is one of the most powerfully effective treatments for mental health.[29] Jogging, running, walking, aerobics, and therapy were the next effective treatments on the list. I appreciated scientist and author Erik Hoel's interpretation, "It's not that exercise beats out SSRIs for depression treatment, but that *just* dancing has the largest effect of *any treatment* for depression. That's kind of beautiful."[30] So cue the music and put on your dancing shoes. This shouldn't surprise us since God's Word says,

> You turned my lament into dancing;
> you removed my sackcloth
> and clothed me with gladness.[31]

The Help of Nature

Want to know another thing that helps our bodies *and* our souls? Getting out into God's creation. Being in nature helps us decompress, unplug, and detox while appreciating God's creation. We must see ourselves rightly as smaller and humbler and see God as larger, and grander. Like John the Baptist said, "He must increase, but I must

---

29. Alicia Fong Yan, Leslie L. Nicholson, Rachel E. Ward, et al., "The Effectiveness of Dance Interventions on Psychological and Cognitive Health Outcomes Compared with Other Forms of Physical Activity: A Systematic Review with Meta-analysis," *Sports Med* 54 (January 25, 2024): 1179–1205, https://doi.org/10.1007/s40279-023-01990-2.
30. @erikphoel, "They buried the lede [sic] on this new study," X (formerly Twitter), February 21, 2024, https://x.com/erikphoel/status/1760338273153568956?s=20.
31. Psalm 30:11

decrease."[32] When we step outside of the things man made and value the nature God made, it reminds us of our place and His. When we look out at a mountain range, seashore, or arboretum, it reminds us of the One who is much greater than us. A 2023 study shows that thirty minutes of nature exploration in green or blue spaces, three to four times a week decreases anxiety and lowers the need for medication by 33 percent.[33] For me, when in nature, I find having high thoughts of God and His truth come easier. Sometimes the physical crowding of being in a city that's very busy, along *with* a busy mind, feels like everything is crowding in. Having the space, not only for our mind but for our bodies, helps us slow down and think clearer. I'm sure you've noticed this after a long walk or admiring a sunset. There's something about witnessing the world God made that helps to rein in your thoughts and put your soul at ease.

> The heavens declare the glory of God,
> and the expanse proclaims the work of his hands.[34]

> "Consider how the wildflowers grow: They don't labor or spin thread. Yet I tell you, not even Solomon in all his splendor was adorned like one of these.[35]

> For his invisible attributes, that is, his eternal power and divine nature, have been clearly seen since the creation of the world, being understood through what he has made.[36]

> When I observe your heavens,
> the work of your fingers,

32. John 3:30
33. Anu W. Turunen et al., "Cross-sectional associations of different types of nature exposure with psychotropic, antihypertensive and asthma medication," *Occupational and Environmental Medicine* 80, no. 2 (2023), doi.org/10.1136/oemed-2022-108491.
34. Psalm 19:1
35. Luke 12:27
36. Romans 1:20

the moon and the stars,
which you set in place,
what is a human being that you remember him,
a son of a man that you look after him?[37]

Every Part of Us

Since we are spiritual, physical, emotional, and mental beings, God provides a variety of support and resources. We can make use of these tools and praise God for them. We are to honor and love God with our whole being, even if anxious. When we talk about loving God with our entire self, to love is *agapáō*, which means actively doing what *the Lord* prefers, *with* Him (by His power and direction). It's that which the Lord has ordained you to do, while considering your season of weakness and possible limitations. So, if our brain is cloudy, and our body constrained and trembling, we love God in faith according to our ability because this is who God has made us to be. Not just loving God in our soul, but with our mind and body too. When all of who we are trembles—our body and mind because of anxiety, and our soul because we are in awe of our God—we rest in the fact that He has created us and is in control of our every circumstance. He has given graces to help supply our needs, and we must not reject the help. We glory in His provision and care. He has not made us merely a soul. We are body *and* soul—both of which He ministers to in His great love, and both of which we give back to Him in holistic worship.

37. Psalm 8:3–4

CHAPTER 8

Jesus Take the Wheel!

Being in a car during a torrential downpour is terrifying. The heavy rain taps on the car's exterior like a herd of wild horse hooves slapping the dark, brisk pavement. We are in the backseat. Our cheeks pressed against the window, and our pupils opened wide. Distressed. We are looking to gauge the stature of the storm and measuring the moment with each convulsive glance. Thunder shouts aloud alongside light that cracks through the sky. Water teems on the road. It parts as the car wheels move through, creating waves and white sprays that jet out from the motion of the tires. Wind flexes its power, rocking the car from side to side. Suddenly, we are aware of our infinitesimal position compared to nature's grand display of dynamism. This is a frightening moment. What makes all the difference is who is in the driver's seat.

Anxiety is the traveling partner all the time for some of us and some of the time for all of us. Although he may be with us during the ride, if he is in the driver's seat, he is a pernicious chauffeur. His unpredictable ways spin and twist us into a frenzy. We tell ourselves that the way to maintain control is through worrying. Worry, though, never helps us manage our present concerns. What worry does is tell us to focus upon our lack while keeping our eye on the future. This just makes us worry more. To feel secure, we become backseat drivers with our minds set on the storm, tempted to make "control" our god in the driver's seat. We convince ourselves that if *we* were driving, things would feel much safer. We think the more "in control" we feel over our lives, the less anxious we will be. We think if we could just switch places with anxiety and finally get ahold of the steering wheel, everything would calm down. The truth is, neither anxiety nor our self-control is going to cut it. We need another driver entirely.

When anxiety takes the wheel, he makes us feel out of control. We feel anxious and vulnerable due to the constant uncertainty of where our thoughts and bodies will or do bring us. We are always on edge because we do not know if our next thought will be followed by twenty more or if that racing heart will snowball into a complete panic attack at 1:00 a.m. To cope, we fight anxiety's feeling of being out of control with the anxiety of being in control. Ultimately, we fight anxiety with more anxiety. The initial anxiety is evident, but this coping mechanism is hidden. However, the source is the same. The desire to possess some sense of control or predictability causes us to think that we are the most qualified driver. There are three ways we handle things when anxiety is driving: obsessively controlling our circumstances, excessively controlling our bodies, and rigidly controlling our boundaries.

Controlling Our Circumstances

As you probably already know, the idol of control has us curating our life in our minds. We struggle to function if things are not exactly how we think our environment should be. Our rigid expectations not only bind the people around us, but bind us as well. We put limits upon the natural responses we come across. In my own life, during the thick of my struggle with anxiety, I tried to control my husband's driving. He would drive the speed limit, but it seemed too fast from the passenger's seat. If I were moving at the same speed, I would feel comfortable, but the moment he was driving, I was confident we would get into an accident. I trusted in *myself* and *my* ability to drive. The moment I experienced discomfort, I was quick to discount Shai's way as unacceptably inferior to my plan. I assigned too much weight to my own strategies and preferences, as if I were the only thing strong enough to get us through a car ride. And yet, as it turned out, Shai's driving skills got us through the journey fine.

Anxiety can also intimidate us into over-planning and over-preparedness. We overthink through all the possibilities, weighing all that could go wrong and researching each detail. We trust that the way we see things is right because we've invested the most time considering each situation from every angle. The assumption is that we care the most of those around us. We quietly affirm ourselves as being the most caring friend, the most caring spouse, the most caring parent, the most caring sibling, and the most caring employee. We make our anxious responses a type of righteousness. We perceive that others underestimate risk and then conclude that they are not as caring nor to be trusted the way we are. But this approach puts pressure on yourself to be bigger, better, and stronger than others around you. Bigger, better, and stronger than you are.

When I was nine, I remember my mother taking me on car rides throughout Hollywood. My mother loved driving fast and stopping five or fewer feet behind a car. She would pump the brakes, and I hated it. I was terrified of getting in an accident. One day, she decided we would drive through the Hollywood Hills. These hills are filled with windy roads, quick curves, and narrow lanes. It was late at night—pitch black minus the streetlights outlining the sidewalk and the headlights. I was so nervous that I would duck down on the floor in the back seat, in the dark, almost in a fetal position. I was bracing myself and praying that we would make it home safely. As a child, it was easy for an adult to dismiss my concerns. I mean, I didn't know how to drive. From her vantage point, she was in control. Although keenly observant, I was limited in understanding all that transpired on the road. But my fears were valid. Years later, when riding with my husband, I felt the same angst, yet this was not the same situation. My anxiety in the car with Shai was not based upon anything my husband was doing but based upon my experience of being terrified as that nine-year-old. At times, when in a heightened state of anxiety while my husband is driving, it's like I'm that child trying to regulate my circumstances. I'm just looking for safety.

Regulating our circumstances by taking control of them appears to be a way to freedom, but it can lead to bondage. Anxiety lies to us and tells us if we take control then we will be better off. But that is not entirely true. Sometimes, thinking of all the possibilities can be a way to prepare well. But other times, *over*thinking all the possibilities is a way to functionally act like we are God, all-seeing, all-knowing, and all-powerful. As I shared in chapter 1, when faced with my fear of dying during my panic attacks, I felt out of control in my mind and body in those moments. It felt like my feet were lifted from the ground, like I was taking steps on the moon, nothing felt bound by gravity. Finding a place to safely rest felt impossible. I thought my endless list of what-ifs—my obsessive thoughts to see and prepare for catastrophe—would help me feel grounded but they never did. They only thrust me further out. None of this means it's wrong to plan something, use your own agency, or own your part to play in the circumstances of life. All those things are well and good, but it matters who is in the driver's seat—meaning, who is bearing the full weight of all those things working out?

Controlling Our Bodies

When anxiety is behind the wheel, not only do we try to control our circumstances, we try to control our bodies. It is important to be in tune with your body's sensations and needs. It is crucial to pick up on physical cues to help you navigate proper physical health. If your head is constantly hurting, you should not ignore it. If your body is telling you something is going on, you want to listen and address it. This is important because sometimes those of us who care for others the most, care for ourselves the least. In fact, learning to pay attention to your body is a big part of recovering from chronic anxiety. Anxiety is often displayed with certain physiological reactions, and there are helpful ways to help your body calm down when it's undergoing those reactions (see Appendix 2 for a breathing technique).

Whether by eating nutritious foods, exercising, taking certain medications, or taking time to rest, there is great value in caring for our bodies. If we don't take adequate time for wellness, then we tell our bodies we will eventually make time for illness. After all, they are the temple of God's Spirit.[1] But anxiety takes the wheel when we move from caring for our body's physical, mental, and emotional health by trying to obsessively control them. Caring for our bodies in service to God shows we revere God, and we are thankful to God for the gift of our bodies. In contrast, controlling our bodies points to the fact that we revere ourselves and put the power to control things in our own hands rather than God's hands. Controlling the body looks different for all of us, but if our bodily attentions are laden with anxiety or obsessiveness, we can suspect we have crossed the line into the driver's seat trying to be our own all-powerful and sovereign God. Here are some examples:

- Hypervigilant symptom-checking on WebMD, Google or other sites
- Hypochondria
- Refusing to serve our family and neighbor because our anxiety causes us to prioritize self-preservation above loving others
- Obsessive calorie counting and or gym workouts that lead to self-condemnation and persistent concern with body weight
- Addictive cosmetic surgeries
- Overspending on cosmetic products or supplements promising a youthful appearance

If any of these resonate deeply with you, I suspect you experience surges of anxiety while you participate in them (and if any of these are quite severe for you, see Appendix 3). For me, that first bullet point has been a struggle. Maybe you can relate. When our body is constantly out of control, and we feel symptoms, aches, and pains all day, it's easy to be hypervigilant about ourselves. We go from ignoring our needs, to only seeing our needs. Every discomfort, tingle, or trouble is a cause to body-watch, because the concern is that if our heart rate increases, it will snowball into another sleepless night, or that throbbing pain

1. 1 Corinthians 6:19

might be cancer. This helicopter body-watching creates a tunnel vision that doesn't allow us to see what God is doing. When we only see the potential difficulty waiting around the corner, we will never see God in our circumstances, nor will we ever be used by God to comfort others through our circumstances.[2] Anxiety, though it may have come upon us through suffering we can't control, can end up making us self-absorbed this way. For example, we do not think about serving that new member after church because we're afraid of overwhelming symptoms that might bombard us if we do.

This does not mean we pretend as though our difficulties do not exist. There is so much space for the seasons when God calls us to completely rest and limit our service. That's part of my own story, and I did it out of faith to God and honor to my body and family. In other seasons, though, He has slowly called me back into ministry, even with the thorn of anxiety still in my side. I learned what serving those around me looked like in what seemed like little ways, with the strength God provided. I learned to believe the truth that "Whoever gives even a cup of cold water to one of these little ones because he is a disciple, truly I tell you, he will never lose his reward."[3]

I cannot know if God is calling you to take a step back or if He is calling you to take a small step toward lifting your eyes upward and being the hands of Christ to your neighbors. What I do know is this: If you try to exercise complete control over your body in the process, you'll never leave your house. Because headaches and unhealthy meals and tiring nights come to all those in service to God[4]—those with anxiety issues and without them. There's no way around it, even for the most vigilant of us. There is a place for stepping back, but you don't want to turn inward forever. To come back out into the world (or into the church) means you accept that you cannot control all the things that might affect your body.

I do not know which season you are in or what environments are most triggering for your body, but the Spirit of God is your help

2. 2 Corinthians 1:3–4
3. Matthew 10:42
4. 2 Corinthians 11:26–27

in discerning where He is calling you. I mentioned going through a season where I was in bed for weeks and although I tried to serve my family, I needed to rest. Talk about not being able to control my body! Then slowly the Lord brought me out of that season, and I had a bit more capacity—not to overwhelm myself by throwing things on my plate, but to wisely discern where I was now compared to where I was before. There were questions I had to answer honestly: Had the season of bed rest passed? Was I still protecting myself (and my time) because I truly needed to rest a little longer, or because I was simply afraid? Was I afraid that those around me would ignore my needs or be disappointed in my lower capacity when I stepped back into the world? Your questions will look different than mine, but it's helpful to work through these with a trusted, godly, and honest counselor or friend as you discern the right next step for your body and your time.

John says to Gaius, "Dear friend, I pray that you are prospering in every way and are in good health, just as your whole life is going well" (3 John 2). John then goes on to commend how Gaius is walking faithfully, welcoming Christians who passed through, and serving and supporting the church. What does this teach us? That we do not have to fear that serving others will compete with our prospering. In His ministry to us and His development of us, God makes room to tend to our inward physical needs *and* grow us in our outward service to others.

Controlling Our Boundaries

Boundaries are wise and helpful, yet not to be worshipped. Our current culture loves rules and drawing the line. This is fine when appropriate, but if God calls us to serve lovingly and we are set on firm, rigid boundaries, it may cause us to rebel against God. Consider Jonah as an example.

Jonah had a hard line against the Assyrians. In today's terms, they were triggering for him. He did not want to preach to Nineveh about the opportunity to receive God's mercy if they repented. His boundaries led him to disobedience, which caused him to run away from the call of God. He was furious that God would choose to display mercy to an undeserving people. It was a hard lesson, but he had to learn that God sometimes calls His followers into territory they would otherwise draw a line around. Likewise, as Christians, we are not our own. We belong to God. We can draw helpful boundaries in our life, but if God asks us to look outward beyond a line we've drawn and into uncomfortable or burdensome territory, we can do what He has called us to in the strength He provides. And we can do it while caring for our spiritual, mental, physical, and emotional needs. Again, this requires discernment on whether God is calling you toward something or something else is. If it's God, the discomfort and burden will be carried by Him, and as you pour out, He'll fill you back up. As you minister to the world, God will minister to your heart and tend to your soul. Like Paul, you'll be able to say, "I am poured out as a drink offering" and "I am fully supplied" at the same time.[5] So, what do your boundaries look like lately? Do not discount that God might be asking you to serve someone else, despite your own anxieties.

Finding Safety in the Fear of God

How do we get anxiety out of the driver's seat? As I said before, we need another driver entirely. I have a friend from the South who cannot deal with snow. Where she comes from, if one snowflake falls on the ground, the entire town shuts down. Snow days, for her, feel okay for a few days, but if they last longer than expected, an anxious realization emerges, "We've got to get to a store for more food and supplies . . . which means we have to drive." For all her life, being behind a wheel while snow and ice are on the ground is a recipe for panic. To this day, if she has to drive in snow, she can barely get to the store without either fishtailing or hyperventilating at the thought of fishtailing. All of that changed though when she married a guy from Pittsburgh. For him, driving through snow was as ordinary as breathing. "It's just something you learn how to do in the North," he told her. Now when

5. Philippians 2:17; 4:18

a snowstorm hits and they have to brave the roads for some reason, she darts to the passenger side. Her husband hops in the driver's seat and gets them where they need to go. His level of skill when it comes to snow has a calming effect on her. If he's in the driver's seat, she knows she's far safer than she would be on her own. He knows what to do, and he's happy to do it.

Something similar is at play when it comes to trusting God. When we lean into fear, what we're really after is control. And underneath the control, what many of us seek is safety. The desire to be safe is natural, and in a world filled with dangers, there is only one place to be safe. And that is in God Himself. When we fear *Him* by revering Him, when we assign *Him* all the weight He's due, when we put *Him* in the driver's seat, we can make it through any terrain.

Why is this so hard for some of us? Because some of us, myself included, were raised in conditions where we were left not to feel safe. We had to fend for ourselves. When we experienced that lack of physical, emotional, or spiritual safety at home, we couldn't physically run away or fight back. Throughout this book I've described the various ways this played out in my story. As I look back on those memories, I see a child who didn't want to be in control; she just wanted to feel safe.

Our safety must be in God Himself since He is our safe place when tumultuous trials are near. We must be all wrapped up and intertwined in His safe presence. Our circumstances cause the realization that we can't rest in them; we can only and always rest in God. We are safe in Him, not because He will always miraculously deliver us out of our trials, but because He will always be there *with us* if we trust Him. He is our shelter and sustenance. Actual safety is found in Him, and we are safe in our gospel identity—in our position as His people. Our identity in Christ is secure because of the One driving us. Here's the truth: We are never actually in control, even when we deceive ourselves and think we might be. The storm is raging, and our Father knows how to drive and navigate us through it. We may be tempted to take the wheel, but the only secure One who can provide sufficient navigation is our sovereign God. When He is in control, we can securely rest in Him.

As for me, I've made up my mind. God was on the throne back when that deer jumped in front of our minivan while driving on the freeway, and He is on the throne now. Despite the fears that show up when I'm in the car or when someone else is driving or when something feels outside my comfort or control, I can trust that God is the One who has full control of the steering wheel. With His voice and presence guiding us, we will arrive safely home.

CHAPTER 9

Job, His Friends, and My Friends

Several years ago, before my personal bout with anxiety, a roommate confided in me about her struggle with anxiety and panic attacks. One day she humbly came to me seeking help. I looked at her like she was a neon green alien reporting her experience of living on a foreign planet in a foreign language. But I was living on *Earth*, where things like anxiety, panic attacks, spiraling thoughts, and fears are met with finger-to-lip. Anxi—*Shush!* We don't say that word around here.

At the time, my (unfortunate) response to my roommate was, "You just need to trust the LORD!" I looked down on her like she was a sick and stress-filled peasant disrupting me, while I was the queen-doctor perched on my throne of peace. "How dare she speak of anxiety in *my* Christian presence?" I pulled out my invisible stethoscope and shared with her some Scriptures on the topic as though they were a prescription: "Take two of these verses each day, and watch anxiety roll off your back like raindrops off a waterproof windbreaker." As I gave her these verses, I gave myself a self-righteous pat on the back. I. fixed. her. Not knowing that, like the parable, I was the Pharisee, and she was the tax collector. I was sure she was in deep sin, and I could see through her heart. I gave the right answer, I thought. I was more spiritual, I thought. While I luxuriated in my celebratory confetti, she didn't seem impressed, as the sizable raindrops were not rolling off. She was dripping wet in anxiety and panic. I didn't notice that part so much. At the time, what I was whispering in the depths of my heart was, "Get over it." *Just trust God*: A simple solution for a simple problem, right? Ah, how I wish that were the case.

In the throes of my trembling journey, I was in bed for three weeks dealing with anxiety's side effects. If I stood for more than fifteen minutes, I felt faint or dizzy and needed to lie down. I also had constant headaches. My stomach was a wrung towel. Rather than try to stand or join my family around our pill-shaped walnut table, I was forced to lay down in a square bed and be okay with that. While in bed, I read several books on anxiety, trials, and suffering—most of them by Christian authors. I was encouraged by some but discouraged by most. One thing I noticed in the Christian books was that there was an emphasis on me being the stronger, better, more courageous version of myself. Cue the jazz hands, glitter, and "you can do it" banners. I was told that all I needed to do was pray harder, read my Bible more, and attempt to conquer my anxieties via an extreme activity like bungee jumping or skydiving. I could barely stand, and they wanted me to jump out of a plane?! Oh, and I must chop down my anxious thoughts like they are floating melons in a game of Fruit Ninja. (Don't misunderstand; we are called to take thoughts captive,[1] but even that can be done anxiously.)

What it seems these authors didn't understand was that every activity feels like an extreme sport when you are lying in bed trembling. Making dinner was an extreme activity. Standing up was an extreme activity. Simply *breathing*, in some cases, was an extreme activity. Also, a lack of Bible reading and/or drop in my belief in God was not the reason for my anxiety journey, as some of the authors suggested. I was not at all doubting God. Remember this started with an accident—an event completely out of my control.

Let me stop and clarify: The advice of reading the Bible and praying is good advice. Christians in the past and present have run to the truths of the Scriptures, even in their persecutions and dying breaths, just like Jesus did on the cross.[2] Christians in the past and present also leaned into prayer all the more earnestly during times of suffering, just like Jesus did in His most agonizing moments.[3] The problems with

1. 2 Corinthians 10:5
2. Matthew 27:46
3. Luke 22:44

this advice are the lack of many other emotional, physical, and mental factors that might also be needed to reduce anxiety, along with the assumption that a simple Bible-reading or prayer session can cure a person's anxiety on the spot.

Another piece of advice in these Christian books that I found harmful was to suggest that there is always a specific sin causing the anxiety. I tried digging for sin like a child taking a shovel to the seashore. Thinking if I could find how far my depravity goes, then maybe that would be the key to untapped victory. Each time I prayed; I trusted that if there were some hidden sin, it would reveal itself. I wanted to identify the sin so I could repent and no longer suffer. The more I dug, to my surprise, I kept coming up empty-handed. It's not that I had no remaining indwelling sin in my heart or suddenly became perfect, rather, there was no sinful stronghold in my life that I could attribute to the anxiety. I couldn't understand why anxiety was so prominent in my life and at the same time, God was not allowing more of my sin to be revealed. I mean, I'm feeling anxious each day, month after month for years. I battled with this tension and questioned what God was doing. What I had to settle in was that overall, what I was going through was not the result of me missing the mark, but the result of actual trauma I experienced in my body. I realized over time that this anxious search for sin as though it were hidden treasure was the wrong focus because it was taking me away from my actual treasure: Jesus.

On top of coming up empty-handed in my sin search, I also came up empty-handed with sympathizers—with friends who truly understood what I was going through. One of the challenges of that season was being misunderstood by others. On the outside I appeared fine, and yet I was not okay. Since many of my friends had not experienced anything like this, it was hard for them to comfort me. I had earnest friends who treated me much the same way I had treated my anxious roommate. Too often we (and those who love us) are looking for our quick fix. Friends don't want us to suffer so they act as a prosperity preacher, riling us up to tell us that if we have enough faith it will zap all our fears away. They want us to line up so they can lay hands, smear an olive oil cross, and declare anxiety is defeated. I wanted this quick fix too, until the Lord showed me, in the middle of my anxiety, that I could have so much more. Even if anxiety never escaped me. If this bully became the thorn in my flesh to taunt me all my days. When I embraced anxiety head-on, not to "get over it," but to seek God in it, things began to change, or I should say, *I* began to change. God showed me how to journey through and how to be more compassionate with my friends when their struggle is different than mine.

So, there I was, unable to blame my anxiety on a specific sin. Being misunderstood and misadvised by friends. Unable to cure my trembling with a quick memory verse. As it turns out, I wasn't alone. There's someone in Scripture who went through a similar experience, and that's Job.

Remember My Servant Job

The theme in Job is unmerited suffering. Job was a righteous man who later became an anxious man because of all that he suffered and lost. We see in his life what so many of us believers can relate to: two realities—righteousness and angst held in tension. The book of Job shows us that we can experience great mental, physical, and spiritual suffering without it always being the result of the sufferer's sin. It teaches us how the enemy's advances and accusations against the righteous may greatly impact us, but they will not ultimately defeat us. Job also reminds us of the important role friends have in discerning the needs of their suffering godly friends.

Scripture says that Job suffered because he was righteous. As a sufferer and a sufferer's friend, it is important for us to expand our minds to create room for this category. Suffering does not automatically mean one has sinned. And living righteously certainly does not mean one will never endure hardship. Even though Job pursued a righteous lifestyle, he still faced traumatic circumstances as a result of living not only in a fallen world, but a fallen world that's still under the sway of the evil one.[4] He maintained his fear of God and yet still experienced the thing he feared.[5]

Despite our familiarity with Job, we struggle with this idea of righteous suffering. Job suffered loss, failed health, and angst, not because he was unfaithful to God but because Satan hated how faithful he was to God. The enemy sought to make Job stumble by removing the blessings in his life. Satan thought that as Job suffered these terrible pains, he would blaspheme God. Satan suggested that Job served God only because God had hedged him in and blessed him with good things in this life. Satan believed when those things were taken away, it would prove that all Job really wanted was what God could give rather than God Himself.

Satan's first attempt to get Job to walk away from God was by taking away his wealth and his dearly loved children. When Job does not curse God, Satan comes back a second time, asking God if he can turn up the heat by afflicting Job's body. As Job is afflicted with sores, he scrapes his wounds with broken pottery. This tremendous suffering ultimately puts a wedge between Job and his wife as she denounces their shared faith. Satan clearly got ahold of her too, as she tells her husband to "curse God and die!"[6] rather than suffer like this.

While the suffering was terrible, one thing is true about Job's story and ours: When the bountiful goods of our lives are stripped away, it exposes our motives for following God. Like a tipped glass, adversity reveals the inner liquid that rested in the cup, the inner workings of the heart. When Satan was allowed to tip over Job's life, the contents showed. Suffering didn't make Job righteous. Job's suffering exposed he was already righteous.

When Job's friends Eliphaz, Bildad, and Zophar heard about what happened to Job, they initially responded well. They met together to sympathize and comfort him. When they saw him from a distance, they did what good friends do; they showed signs of mourning and solidarity by weeping, tearing their robes, and throwing dust. They

4. 1 John 5:19
5. Job 3:25
6. Job 2:9

sat on the ground with him for seven days and seven nights and said nothing because his suffering was so intense. They wept because their friend was weeping. They waited until Job spoke. They didn't try to break the silence with awkward and clichéd explanations (at least not initially). They listened as Job achingly and vulnerably said, "Naked I came from my mother's womb, and naked I will leave this life. The LORD gives, and the LORD takes away. Blessed be the name of the LORD."[7]

Job was naked, stripped down to his bare essence, without his family, health, or wealth. He was confronted with his own weakness, powerlessness, and smallness. Job believed if there was a mediator who could stand between him and God, then his case would be heard and the affliction would stop. Job's affliction shows us, and his lament tells us, that one of the purposes of affliction is to lead us to our own humanity, which then causes us to look for a mediator. Job wondered how he could reach God. He knew he could not stand in God's courtroom alone. In Job's third speech to God, he says, "There is no mediator between us, to lay his hand on both of us."[8] He was looking for someone to argue his case before God and stop his suffering. Of course, the person he was aching for was not one of his friends but Christ, who would eventually come to not only mediate between man and God, but to fully and finally end the enemy's attacks on the children of God. But that day hadn't come yet.

Job's Friends

Job's friends started out sitting beside him and grieving with him but after listening awhile, they do what fallen friends do—what we all do at some point or another. They fill the awkward and sad silence with speculation. And so, Job had to bear with his friends as they pontificated on what was commonly believed about suffering in the ancient Near East—which, honestly, isn't all that different than the

7. Job 1:21
8. Job 9:33

way religious folks try to approach suffering in our own day. Much like many of us, they believed the reason Job suffered was because something was awry within Job. They couldn't identify a specific sin Job committed, but they were fixated upon the fact that there must be *something* he needed to repent of. Once he appeased God by turning from the sin, they believed Job would be restored.

It wasn't that Job's friends *always* said false things while counseling him. Many things they said were true. The problem with their words was that they were not appropriate or timely since they didn't apply to Job's specific situation. In short, Job's friends counseled him repeatedly to just *find the sin and repent of it already.* That's not always bad advice; sometimes people are suffering in a miserable situation and it really *is* due to their own sin. I think of Nathan approaching David, for example, when David was in adulterous sin up to his eyeballs.[9] He needed someone to tell him to repent. But Job's friends weren't dealing with David. They were dealing with the opposite—a man who made a covenant with his eyes to not look on a woman to lust.[10] Job was not struggling with a sinful stronghold in his life. Therefore, their counsel, which assumed Job had sinned, was not appropriate to the situation. You tell someone in sin to repent. You tell a sufferer something different.

What can we learn from this? There are times when we may be tempted to copy and paste an answer to different people without considering their individual needs. When we speak a well-intentioned but untimely word that does not appropriately apply, it becomes a deeper source of hurt and discouragement for our suffering friend. What we say makes a huge difference in whether we will be a friend who is supportive and strengthening or a friend who introduces more chaos, furthering the sufferer's isolation.

Discernment is vital to caring for our anxious friends. Even if we have experienced anxiety ourselves, it doesn't mean that our friends are mimicking our affliction. We cannot put a one-size-fits-all Band-Aid upon all our anxieties, which means, with the Spirit's guiding help, we

9. 2 Samuel 12
10. Job 31:1

must do the work of figuring out the person we are dealing with in each conversation. Even if we have multiple "Jobs" in our lives, no two are the same. Helping and supporting the various Jobs in your life will look as diverse as each one of their faces and stories.

I've asked four of my friends to share their own unique experiences with different forms of anxiety. I want you to hear from Elisabeth, Trent, Sasha, and Lisa because their stories are different than mine. Maybe you relate to them, or their story will help you think about the person in your life you are called to sit with.

Hearing from My Friends

My friend Elisabeth recently shared how, as a child and young adult, she struggled with scrupulosity (a form of obsessive-compulsive disorder [OCD], another type of anxiety disorder). Elisabeth's condition would cause her to pray the same prayers repeatedly, hundreds of times in one sitting. This behavior is a hypervigilant interpretation of praying without ceasing. Listen as she shares:

> My experience is of a subtype of obsessive-compulsive disorder and can also be called Moral OCD or Religious OCD. Guilt over imagined sins or intrusive thoughts gets my brain stuck in a loop. That's the obsessive part. Because these thoughts terrify me, I turn to rituals to cope. That's the compulsive part. Caught in this cycle, I'm not praying or repenting in healthy ways. I am trying to keep myself safe before God in my own strength. I'm often in search of sin to confess—even if it was imagined sin. When I suffered with this, I unnecessarily apologized to others and meticulously confessed my sins to God. That was how I kept myself safe. Over time and with much faltering, I began to resist walking the maze of scrupulosity. Though I couldn't quiet the obsessions, I could refuse to engage in the compulsions. This

> is how scrupulosity's grip was loosened—acting as though I'm safe even when my feelings and thoughts say otherwise. The lens through which I had been understanding salvation was focused inward—on my heart—instead of upward—on Christ's work. My standing with God is dependent on Jesus's perfection, not mine. I learned to look at Christ each time my assurance wavered. Joining a church where we found pastors, elders, and church members who not only acknowledged the reality of mental illnesses, but actively encouraged conversation about this difficult topic was helpful. It was here that I began to share my struggles and found the courage to schedule an appointment at an anxiety clinic where I was finally diagnosed with obsessive-compulsive disorder.
>
> The road to healthy management is still full of ups and downs, doubts and fears. I am helped by pastors whose preaching is mindful of both hardened *and* overly sensitive consciences amongst their listeners. Therapy and medication equip me to recognize intrusive thoughts and discount obsessive fears. As someone who navigates scrupulosity daily, I am blessed by therapy, medication, a supportive church family, praying friends, and a patient husband. But, most of all, God's greatest gift to me is Himself. There is a person outside of me in whom I can hope when all else seems lost. That person is Jesus, and He is always enough.

Meet an elder at my church, Trent, who struggles with prolonged anxiety.

> As I think back to my childhood days, I realize I was always prone to anxiety in certain situations. However, it was the latter part of 2020, during the pandemic, where I started to experience prolonged

anxiety. I could go from feeling fine one week to feeling terribly anxious the next. What made it worse was even in the periods of feeling fine, there was always a worry of, "when is the anxiety coming back?" It was like I had this unwanted visitor who would make himself at home in my mind for days at a time, disappear, and then come back. For the most part I could still hide the distress and move along slowly with my daily routine. But my wife and kids noticed something was off. I dropped about twenty-five pounds and would go through periods where I'd only eat once a day, and even then, I was just force-feeding myself. Sleep became my enemy as I would often wake up at night, lay there worried, being unable to find any rest.

Severe anxiety may be embarrassing, but the help I needed far outweighed my pride. So I gradually increased my circle of help. I asked for prayer and support from a few fellow elders and especially drew near to one of them who had experience in counseling and mental health. This was emotionally freeing as I was shown compassion and had folks walk beside me during the mental fog. It didn't always make the anxiety go away, but it lifted me spiritually as I felt the comfort of their prayers and petitions to God on my behalf. This was a means of grace I was now experiencing in a new way as I fought through the anxiety.

I also sought out a fellow congregant who specialized in mental health and medication. Up to this point I was not open to medication because I thought it would be addictive and cause me to lose my clarity of thought, which is humorous considering where my mind was at the time. But at my wife's encouragement I met with this person. She explained to me that most SSRIs (antidepressant medication) are not addictive, and to tell my doctor I don't want "habit-forming"

> medication. Up to this point, although my doctor recommended I seek therapy and start a dose of antidepressants, I was not in favor of the medication. Plus, doesn't taking medication mean my faith is weak?
>
> It was through a panel[11] where I heard a mother talk about her thought process on medication that I began to consider it for myself. I knew there was nothing to be ashamed about concerning medication. Yes, we can take medication too far and should invite others into our lives to wisely think through it. But medication is also a common grace from God in which we can be thankful for as believers.
>
> The doctor prescribed me a low-dose antidepressant that I took for three years. In God's kindness with therapy, medication, and care from other believers, I haven't experienced a panic attack in years or found myself back in that severe state of anxiety. Do I still sometimes go through low levels of anxiety? Yes, and there could be rougher days of anxiousness ahead. However now I have a new perspective as God has given me tools to better respond to anxiety.

Another friend of mine, Sasha, struggles with social anxiety.

> My first panic attack happened in church. I was fifteen or sixteen at the time. My mother and I visited a new church much larger than our previous one. I recall the triggering moment when an usher asked us to move from our seat in the back, all the way up to the second row. The walk to that second row before curious faces felt long and menacing. By the time I sat down, my heart had begun beating rapidly from my chest. I was hyperventilating, and tears stung

11. Jackie Hill Perry, Jasmine Holmes, and Melissa Kruger, "Fear and Anxiety," *Let's Talk* (podcast), February 12, 2021, https://www.thegospelcoalition.org/podcasts/lets-talk-podcast/lets-talk-fear-and-anxiety/.

my eyes. I had no idea what was happening. I had never experienced anything like this before; I didn't have the language of "anxiety" or "panic attack," and confusion about whether I could be having a real medical emergency only made the situation worse. Thankfully, not long after its onset, the panic subsided and all was well again.

I wouldn't experience this again for another decade when, after moving to a new city and joining a new church, I began having more frequent panic attacks and a constant feeling of anxiety that seemed permanently lodged in my chest. I was encouraged to spend time figuring out what was triggering these attacks, and through journaling I began to. I was living with a lot of pent-up, undealt-with anxiety, which often made it easy for seemingly minor things to inevitably set off a new panic attack. My new lifestyle of having moved from a quiet suburban life where I had ample time to write and read and reflect with God, to a busy life in a major city where my schedule was always booked, was a major contributor to the ongoing anxiety. I would go to work and then come home to a full house, a home I shared with several sisters from my church. I was a part of a beautiful, intentional church community, which for me meant spending several evenings after work in a different prayer meeting, book club, seeking to get to know and spend time with every member, and at one point, three different weekly Bible studies. Even times alone were anxiously spent anticipating the next thing on a long to-do list. After some months I was completely burnt-out without even realizing it.

A conversation with a fellow introverted sister helped to identify even more of what was going on with me. She expressed her displeasure in being an

> introvert, saying we were unable to honor God like our extroverted brethren were more readily equipped to do. Those with the bandwidth and capacity to get much done helped to establish the general way of life for our church. Not being gifted with the same bandwidth often led to feeling misunderstood, overwhelmed, and anxious as I strove to keep up. Thank God for growth in understanding God's perfect design in each of us. What I am unable to do in quantity, I can still do in quality, to the glory of God. This growth in understanding freed me to step back from several responsibilities, honing in on only a few. Over time, finding more meaningful times of rest alleviated so much angst and anxiety in my mind and in my body.

Last, listen to my friend Lisa, a wise pastor's wife. She has not experienced anxiety personally but has walked alongside her child's anxiety.

> Parenting a child with anxiety is one of the hardest things I've ever done. Anxiety in children can take many different forms but it's not the same as normal childhood worries and fears. Everyone understands a child who is nervous the first day of school, but anxiety defies rational explanation. At times my child was so paralyzed by anxiety he was unable to leave the house or even take a shower. Since few people could relate to my parenting struggles their well-intentioned comments and advice often left me feeling isolated. Sometimes their comments were hurtful or judgmental because they assumed I must be doing something wrong, or that my child was merely being defiant. They couldn't fathom why a child would hide under the bed when it was time to leave for a school where he was well-liked and excelling academically. Since

it was hard to explain my struggles with my child's anxiety while maintaining his privacy, it was easier for me to keep quiet about it.

As my child suffered, I suffered. It was difficult watching his distress, knowing there was little I could do to provide relief. It was painful seeing him miss out on opportunities. When the anxiety was at its worst, it was exhausting for me at every level. I was frequently up in the night with my child. I had to be ready at any moment for a call from school, steeling myself as he begged me to pick him up early. I needed to remain steady when the anxiety caused him to spin out of control. I needed to be a safe harbor when nothing in his life felt safe. I struggled with guilt, wondering if there was something I had done or not done that had contributed to this.

Parenting this child was more complex than parenting my other children. When he did something troubling, I couldn't tell if it was because of his sin, anxiety, or spiritual warfare. I wanted my child's behavior to fit into clear categories so I would know exactly how to respond. It was never that neat. Often my child's behavior was a combination of several categories. This complexity required prayer and wisdom from me as a parent. Since anxiety defies logic the normal parenting model of consequences for actions didn't work when anxiety was in control. I had to think more creatively and sympathetically so I could continue to parent faithfully and biblically.

Although I would never wish this on any parent, God used my child's anxiety in my life for spiritual good. When I was plagued by guilt, I reminded myself that "there is no condemnation for those in Christ Jesus" (Rom. 8:1). I spent more time in prayer crying out to the Lord and seeking wisdom. Since

> progress was slow, I often used Scripture to remind myself of God's promises and his proven character. And over time I learned that the Lord uses the brokenness of this world to do his good work. Both my child and I have a deeper sense of God's goodness as a result of this trial.

I am grateful for each of my friend's willingness to share their experiences vulnerably, whether navigating mental health or caring for someone who is in the thick of the battle.

Practical Ways to Care for Our Friends

Author Amy Carmichael said, "If souls can suffer alongside, and I hardly know it, because the spirit of discernment is not in me, then I know nothing of Calvary love."[12] Christ has been attentive to our needs. We must be attentive to the needs of our friends. So many have been hurt in Christian communities because of an unfit word spoken by "Job's friends." Here are a few things to consider before being quick to speak.

Start by showing up and listening

Genuinely ask your friend how they are doing that day and listen. How are their stress levels? Ask them to tell you about the symptoms they face. What's been hard? Don't jump in with sharing how you are doing. Give space for them to share and not feel rushed. Don't be quick to be a "fixer." Be present and ready to listen and mourn with them if it's a hard day, and rejoice with them if it's a better day.[13]

Care for their practical needs

Ask if there is anything practical that you can do to be a good friend to them. Has your friend eaten? Would a meal be helpful?

12. Amy Carmichael, *If* (1938; repr. CLC Publications, 2011).
13. Matthew 26:36–38; Romans 12:15

Maybe they would be served by you taking their child for a playdate while they get a nap. Consider a weekend friend's trip to some blue or green space.

Encourage their worship of God

Could you read their favorite passage of Scripture or gently sing a gospel song or hymn to them? Watch an encouraging Christian film or listen to a sermon together. Another idea is memorizing Scripture together.

Encourage their physical health

You could practice breathing techniques together. We talked about dance—you could encourage a dance party or schedule times to go to the gym together each week to positively impact their mental health. Many people find it easier to share their struggles when they are not in a face-to-face conversation, so taking a walk can make it easier to talk and has the benefits of fresh air, change of scenery, and exercise.

Encourage their rest

How can we encourage our friends to incorporate activities or moments of rest that nourish and revive them when they are weary? How can we encourage Sabbath rest for them on a regular basis?

Be cautious of your words

There is no need to say, "I understand." Unless you are experiencing the same trial, and even still, I'm sure there are some differences. Do not allow "I understand" to be used as a filler when you don't know what to say. I have learned this the hard way. I said it to a grieving friend years ago after she lost her mother. She looked at me and asked, "Oh, you lost your mother too?" At that point I hadn't. I responded "no" and I felt terrible. I spoke quickly and uncarefully. Now I know what it's like to lose my mother and unless you've experienced that, you do not understand. Sufferers are not expecting everyone else to understand, so it's okay if you don't. A better response is, "I'm so sorry.

How have you been coping with that lately?" or "Is there any way I can care for you or meet a practical need?"

Do not minimize anxiety through compliments

People say things like, "You look so put together, though!" or "You sound fine" or "You look fine to me!" Stroking a façade only makes us want to hide behind it all the more.

Keep the gospel central

Remind yourself and your friends that healing from angst is not the reward of their faith and it's not the primary goal. Nor is the goal having the friend you knew prior to their mental health challenges. This trial will certainly change your friend, but the goal is to be more like our Lord in the end. This means that we must remember that God is doing something far greater than the stagnant or seemingly linear plans we have for our friend.

Gentleness is a beautiful virtue that blesses those it meets

If you can be gentle and tender-hearted with your friends, not because you've been in their shoes, but because you love them dearly, it goes a long way. I can say this from experience! I once had an episode of fierce physical trembling in the middle of the night that seemed so bad that I felt the need to call an ambulance. Through a conversation with the kindest and most gentle EMT, we traced the trembling back to some vitamins I had taken right before bed—vitamins with natural stimulants I was supposed to take in the morning. I could have felt embarrassed and ashamed, but the gentle help of this EMT left me encouraged and cared for. When an anxiety-ridden person is not thinking straight, we don't need a person looking at us like we have three heads; we need a person with a big heart who can gently point us to truth.

Coming into the Light

I want to say a brief word to the sufferer about how you can be a good friend to those not suffering. Sometimes the problem isn't the church's leaders or the church's version of "Job's friends." Sometimes, for the anxious person, the problem is simply coming out into the light and admitting to friends and leadership that you're struggling. That was the case for me as well. There were many times I would feel like an anxiety/panic attack was coming over me while doing something like having dinner with friends. I had to learn to whisper prayers to God, asking for help. But that was not all God was calling me to. I often wouldn't want to tell my friends because I didn't want to make the time about me or disrupt the dinner. I would go to the bathroom, splash water on my face, pray, and try to calm myself down quickly. Basically, I was trying to handle my issue with anxiety all by myself. What I learned is that I couldn't. Anxiety would never fit into a little private box for me to tuck away. Actually, this was a way to preserve my pride. I wanted to appear to be fine. I didn't want to be vulnerable and humbled. The problem was that anxiety would peek its head up and out and be loud and disruptive like a preschooler using her outside voice in a library. Eventually, I had no other choice but to welcome my Christian friends into my suffering. I confess this because I hope you won't wait as long as I did to share your suffering. Eventually I would let friends know that I was not feeling well and ask them to pray for me, right then and there. They would and it helped. There is something about not feeling alone in the battle. There is something about exposing the secret monster to light.

If you're a fellow struggler who battles with anxiety, let me encourage you with this: Your church could have the kindest leaders and the best of friends to help you in your journey, but if you don't come out into the light and let them know about your struggle, you'll never experience the power of their presence and involvement. If you are like Job, asking, "Where then is my hope? Who can see any hope for me?"[14] The answer, of course, is the Lord. But it's also the people He's

14. Job 17:15

placed in our lives. Lean into them. A good friend will intercede and answer by pointing to God and saying what I offer you now: "I know the waves are making it difficult to see the way ahead. I will ford the waters with you. Link arms with me and I will hold out hope. I see hope for you, even if you can't right now. I will not settle for cheap phrases and unkind responses. I will honor you, weep with you, and comfort you with the same comfort I have received."

CHAPTER 10

Casting Cares

When we were taking the drive up to Michigan to visit family during the accident, I was going up to visit with my grandmother Mary. She was ninety-two at the time. Though we drove, we usually fly in to visit. Every time I come to town she waits in the airport gate to greet me. As I see her, the first thing she does after giving me a hug and kiss is grab my suitcase. It doesn't matter how heavy the bag is, she grabs it with ninety-plus years of determination. If I refuse to allow her, I will be fussed at. It is her way of loving me after a long flight. What she communicates with her act is that she wants to make use of resources she doesn't think I have but is confident she has. It is her way of lessening my burden by taking on my baggage or cares.

Casting your cares on a person strong enough to handle your cares and anxieties shows us if we understand our capacity or think too highly of ourselves. We're familiar with the command to cast our cares to the Lord in 1 Peter 5:7. Or perhaps we're familiar with a similar passage in Psalm 55:22 which says,

> Cast your burden on the Lord,
> and he will sustain you;
> he will never allow the righteous to be shaken.

I had heard these passages throughout my life. I had memorized them. But never was there a more pressing time to understand them than when I started my journey with anxiety. I was forced to admit that though I was familiar with these passages, I didn't understand them or how they pertained to me. To learn, I asked God to teach me how to give Him every financial, relational, ministerial, and residential care, along with any other care that I was carrying. I remember telling God, "I don't know what it means to cast my cares over to You." I was resistant to give my luggage over to my ninety-two-year-old grandmother, but I was ignorant as to how to give my burdens over to God. I had to ask Him to please show me how. As a generous Father, He helped. He provided the Holy Spirit to assist me in my need,[1] and this time was no exception for me. By the Spirit's working, what I learned was to depend upon God *specifically* and *continually*.

Casting Cares Specifically

Scripture's requirement is that I ask Him for what I need. Not in a general or vague way, but *exactly* what I need. Examples abound of this: The persistent widow in Luke 18 wanted justice for a situation with an adversary. She didn't pray for "world peace," though that's a great prayer. She had a particular situation with an adversary—a particular relationship that was preventing her from justice—and she persisted in asking for that specific situation repeatedly. In a parable in Luke 11, the man who woke up his neighbor in the middle of the night didn't ask for "God to be with us right now" or "safe travels during the holiday season" for his neighbor's family. Again, those are good prayers, but they are general, and they weren't related to the need of the hour for this man. The man who woke up his neighbor asked for bread. Three loaves to be specific. He had unexpected company and had no food to give them, so when he knocked on his neighbor's door, he asked for exactly what he needed—down to the number of loaves! When Peter was thrown in prison in Acts 12, for what exactly did the church pray as they gathered? For good weather? For God's general blessing over the gospel going forward in their city? No. While Peter was "kept in prison," we're told "prayer was made without ceasing of the church unto God *for him*."[2] The prayer for the gospel to go forward is a great prayer, but right now, the specific hindrance to that mission

1. Luke 11:13
2. Acts 12:5 KJV

was that Peter was in prison. So they prayed not just for gospel expansion, but *for Peter.*

So that's what I began to do. I asked God for exactly what I needed every hour. Every minute. Just as Philippians 4:6 contrasts anxiousness with "in everything, through prayer and petition with thanksgiving, present your requests to God," I determined that I would take every instance of angst and pray specifically about it. I was specific with my struggles. I was in such desperation and, at the same time, convinced that the only person who could provide help was God. Whenever there was a care, I would metaphorically bow my head. I could be talking to a friend and feeling anxious, I began to talk to God in my head unbeknownst to them.

Casting your burdens means releasing your cares to God in faith. This means giving the entirety of your concerns to Him in prayer and surrender. It is humbling to acknowledge you cannot carry your burdens because they are too much for you—I know this well because I'm right there with you. Yet, I am convinced that our primary source of help will come from above. I'm convinced that when we release our cares, God really does catch them.

We go back to God. We call out to Him like the infant this trial has exposed us to be. If our motives are off, that's not a death sentence to our relationship with God, for we have a God who helps refine our motives over time and promises to mature us. He might decline to answer a prayer in the way we thought it should be answered, but He'll never decline *us*. We're His children—needy, trembling, and all. And so, we must determine that being needy is not an insufficiency but a lesson in sensibility. And as for that passage in James, well, it actually continues this way: "God resists the proud but gives grace to the humble" (James 4:6). So if you find your prayers aren't all you want them to be and you feel quite low about that, the only thing waiting for you in that lowliness is God's *grace*, not His rejection.

Casting Cares Continually

Casting our cares continually means to cast our cares on God specifically but also persistently. Our cares are continual; therefore, our prayers should also be continual. Since there are many cares, each one provides an opportunity for a connecting point to the One who can handle their substantial weight. Or, as Spurgeon put it:

> Cares are manifold; therefore, let your prayers be as manifold. Turn into a prayer everything that is a care. Let your cares be the raw material of your prayers; and, as the alchemists hoped to turn dross into gold, so do you, by a holy alchemy, turn what naturally would have been a care into spiritual treasure in the form of prayer. Baptize every anxiety into the name of the Father, and of the Son, and of the Holy Ghost, and so make it into a blessing.[3]

Remember the parable of the widow in Luke 18? She didn't only ask the judge for the specific justice; she needed a particular relationship. She "kept coming to him" with this request.[4] To the point that the judge called it "pestering" him and finally decided that "I will give her justice, so that she doesn't wear me out by her persistent coming."[5] Remember the church praying for Peter in prison? It's not just that their prayer was made for Peter in particular. It's that their "prayer was made *without ceasing*."[6] *Kept coming. Pestering. Without ceasing.* The point is this: God wants you to wear Him out with your visits to His throne room.

While we speak to God through prayer, it is also important to be aware of how we are speaking to ourselves. Does your internal monologue sound anything like this?

---

3. Charles Spurgeon, sermon "Prayer, The Cure for Care" (January 12, 1888), *Metropolitan Tabernacle Pulpit Volume 40*, https://www.spurgeon.org/resource-library/sermons/prayer-the-cure-for-care/#flipbook/.
4. Luke 18:3
5. Luke 18:5
6. Acts 12:5 KJV, emphasis added

- What if ________________________________
  ____________________?
- What if ________________________________
  ____________________?
- What if ________________________________
  ____________________?

We can take every "what if" and "if then"—which are really just fears and anxieties—and turn it into a prayer to our God. Here is an example:

> "Lord, I am concerned about what will happen if I die. I feel so much fear. God, would You teach me what Your Word says about death, and comfort me, reminding me of my imperishable hope?"[7]

Choose on "if then" or "what if" statement from above and turn it into your own personal prayer:

____

____

____

____

Life is about distinguishing the "what ifs" from the "what is," and the "if thens" from the "it is." Each of these thoughts and questions regarding fears about the past and/or future swirls us into either low or high levels of anxiety. When the mind is filled with flaming darts, like David we say, "I am restless and in turmoil with my complaint, because of the enemy's words."[8] Whether those words are an acute, loud bark that overwhelms us or a low hum acting as the soundtrack of our life, they often sound similar in our minds but differ based on the source, frequency, and the volume. We can hear and apply David's words in this psalm:

---

7. There are prayer prompts in Appendix 1.
8. Psalm 55:2b–3a

Negative Self-Talk

> *"If I'm anxious, then that shows I am not a faithful Christian."*
>
> *"What if they don't like me, and I'm forced to be alone?"*
>
> *"What if they do like me, and I'm forced to make friends?"*
>
> *"What if I ruin my child's life?"*
>
> *"What if I get cancer?"*
>
> *"What if I die!?"*

We also may have spiritual anxieties. We meditate on c such as,

> *"What if I'm not a Christian?"*
>
> *"Why is my husband's spiritual life waning . . . what if he walks away from God?"*
>
> *"Will my children ever come to Christ? What if they never do?"*

As we pay attention to the scenario, we see that anxiety s us and sometimes sounds more like words from an enemy tha our minds, affecting our lives. And did you notice how each is a projection of the future?

Take a moment to write out any "if then" or "what if" st you are believing right now.

- If ____________________________, then ____________________________.
- If ____________________________, then ____________________________.
- If ____________________________, then ____________________________.

> Cast your burden on the LORD, and he will sustain you;
> he will never allow the righteous to be shaken.[9]

If Christ has made us righteous, we seek His kingdom despite how we feel. Our King receives every care we cast upon Him, especially when those cares are fears. He wants to carry them for us, whether natural fears or sinful fears, whether rational fears or irrational.

Irrational Fears

When one of my children struggles with fear, a question we sometimes ask is: "Is this fear rational or irrational?" An irrational fear is "a phobia, a word that comes from the Greek 'phobos' . . . an irrational fear of something that poses little or no actual danger."[10] These fears may have a low risk of danger and be unlikely to happen, but they cause significant distress nevertheless. For example, we commonly hear about fears of spiders, elevators, clowns, germs, and flying. The truth is any bad thing *can* happen, but often, our high level of concern doesn't match the low probability of it taking place. What I am saying is, living in this world, we have to take some risk. If we can see the low probability of our irrational fears and how they pose little risk to us (or those we love), slowly, we may be able to shake loose from the hold they have on us. This is how I slowly began to drive again. The risk is there and all of the symptoms are too, but I took slow steps in the direction of facing my fear. We must confess along with the old hymn:

> We rest on Thee, our Shield and our Defender;
> We go not forth alone against the foe;
> Strong in Thy strength, safe in Thy keeping tender.
> We rest on Thee, and in Thy Name we go.[11]

9. Psalm 55:22
10. Lucy Ann Moll, "Overcoming a Phobia, Part Two," Biblical Counseling Coalition, September 4, 2020, https://www.biblicalcounselingcoalition.org/2020/09/04/overcoming-a-phobia-part-two/.
11. Edith Gilling Cherry, "We Rest on Thee," (1895). Public domain.

We do not cast our cares and fears upon ourselves or fight in our own strength. We hide ourselves behind our Shield and Defender. He is who fights for us, even if, like Paul, He doesn't remove the thorn from us immediately. God is more concerned about our eternal hope than our physical healing, more interested in cultivating inward virtue rather than bodily victories. Humility is the stripping down from any exalted position we may want God, others, and self to believe about us and viewing ourselves according to God's perspective. Anxiety helps with this. It strips away the ego and forces us to experience the reality of our humanity—weakness, finiteness, and frailty. It transforms us from the delusional, immature, and unprotected soldier into the humble warrior who is wise enough to put on the only protective covering that is strong enough to withstand the world, the flesh, and the devil: Jesus. One may think he is strong enough on his own, only to walk into a bloodbath and find he is actually quite vulnerable. The other knows he is vulnerable to the point of trembling, and in his humility, suits up with the right armor. You tell me who wins the battle in the end—the one trusting in the strength of his own flesh? Or the one who covers himself with the power and protection of a strong, infinite, and perfect Savior?

As I said before, for me, continual prayer sometimes meant every fifteen minutes—or even every minute! Eyes closed, eyes opened, in a conversation, or alone, like a twenty-four-hour conveyor belt at the airport dumping out suitcase after suitcase. I was unloading every care, not upon my ninety-two-year-old grandmother, but upon the One who had even greater sufficient resources to handle my baggage. In one fifteen-minute window, it is quite possible that all these prayers are silently lifted up to God as you flit from one activity to the next:

- "God, my heart is racing, I feel out of control, and like I'm going crazy. Please remind me that You are with me and able to help me through these fears and concerns."
- "Lord, our bank account is low, and I'm tempted to worry. I am worried that we won't have enough money to buy food for the children tomorrow, so

help me trust that You are our provider. Please grant us daily bread since You care for the ravens, and we mean more to You than them."

- "Lord, I feel like giving up because life feels too hard. Suffering is dragging on, and I am weary. Lord, help! Pull me out of this pit of depression and despair."
- "God, I'm discouraged and worried about my prodigal child. Lord, they don't seem to care about You like they once did. I'm concerned about the path they are on. I can't fix them nor control them; they need to have an encounter with You. Help me not to fret."
- "Oh Lord, did You just see this text come through with another request on my time and energy? I feel like I can't make all these things happen—be my strong and steady support. By Your Spirit, help me discern if this request should be answered with a yes or a no. I will automatically say yes without Your guidance, help, and conviction. Give me wisdom even now!"

As a bag is loaded on, you load it off to the Lord. Prayer by prayer, need by need, minute by minute. The world tells us that we are fools to pray and endure suffering. God says that we are fools *not* to depend upon Him for everything.[12] And God is right. Why would we bear the weight when we have a sure, secure, and strong place to unburden ourselves? As each care gets hurled onto you, hurl it on to God. It's not just that He *can* handle when you cast your burdens onto Him; it's that He *wants* you to.

12. Romans 12:12; James 1:2–5

Fighting Anxiety with Thankfulness

Scripture also says to cast these requests, fears, and cares up to God "with thanksgiving."[13] Thanksgiving loosens the chains of fear and anxiety. It is hard to be afraid when you recall the character of Jehovah Jireh.[14] Thanksgiving helps us recall our past deliverances. Even if God has allowed certain forms of suffering in your life that you cannot wrap your mind around, they do not outweigh the mercies of God. Said another way, because of the existence of suffering and burdens in this life, we have a reason to cast our cares on the Lord always. On the flip side, because of the existence of God's mercy, grace, and blessing in this life, we have a reason to "rejoice in the Lord always."[15] It is through thanksgiving that we find the ability to do this.

When you feel overwhelmed with anxieties, spend time reflecting upon what you can be thankful for. It can be something specific He's done for you lately, or a spiritual reality that you are thankful for no matter the specific season of life. Examples include:

- "Lord, I thank You that You have delivered me from my sin and are able to provide for my other needs."[16]
- "God, I thank You that I am in Christ and Your Son has known suffering and therefore is with me in the midst of this challenge."
- "Lord, I thank You for helping us get through that financial obstacle last month."
- "God, I thank You that You are keeping me in my right mind. Thank You for the ability to praise You despite how I feel physically and mentally."

---

13. Philippians 4:6
14. Jehovah Jireh means the Lord will provide, https://biblehub.com/topical/naves/j/jehovah-jireh—mount_moriah,_in_jerusalem,_where_abraham_offered_isaac.htm.
15. Philippians 4:4
16. Romans 8:32

- "God, I thank You that You are using my weakness to make Your strength more evident in my life."
- "Lord, thank You for providing the strength I needed for this workweek. It was heavy and I didn't think I had the capacity to get to Friday. I felt shaky and scattered. But You heard my cries and supplied my strength. I praise You for Your care and concern and provision. You are a God who knows our coming and our going. You are present and active week in and week out. You proved that this week, and I'm so grateful to know I can depend on You for help!"

Even if these prayers don't resonate with you, consider three things that you can be thankful for that are specific to your life this week or month, and write them down. Once you've listed them, don't leave them on the paper. Lift them up to God in a prayer of thanksgiving.

In Philippians 4:7, God says that thankfulness will bring about a peace that "surpasses all understanding," and it will "guard your hearts and minds in Christ Jesus." I believe this is because although thankfulness doesn't cure anxiety wholesale, it *can* break the pattern of anxious thoughts in certain spiraling moments. Anything unpracticed feels unsafe. Once we practice obeying this Scripture, we will glory in the safety and encouragement of gratitude. Appreciativeness takes us from a hyperfocus on our typical ruminating thoughts and helps lift our attention upward to what God has done. As we lift our gaze, we can seek the things above and set our minds on things above.[17] Believers already have the God of peace,[18] but entrusting God with our anxieties through thanksgiving allows us to have the peace of God.[19]

Some may protest here, saying something like "Gratitude lists and one-off Scripture passages are great, but they don't fix something as

17. Colossians 3:1–4
18. Romans 5:1
19. Galatians 5:22

intense as an anxiety disorder." To that I would point back to chapters 7 and 8. Scripture, and its instruction toward gratitude, is certainly not the *only* tool in the toolbox when it comes to handling anxiety, but it certainly deserves to be the most well used. Which means we don't throw it out once we get new tools. We still use the tools we have alongside the new additions. The truth of Philippians 4, for example, may feel like old news—or rather, ancient tools—to some. But it is good news. And I understand that, especially because I come from a background where the only recommendations around anxiety were more Bible and more prayer, and that was it. However, ancient doesn't always mean bad or irrelevant. Ancient can also mean lasting—things that stand the test of time. So, consider passages like Philippians 4 in light of that. The Word is God-breathed and has revived generations of anxious saints. God's Word is the only tool inspired and infallible, that will never return void. For me, when I faced the choice of practicing its ancient wisdom or rolling my eyes at it, I of course made the decision to go with the former. I've learned that when I consistently practice its key passages regarding anxiety, I am not cured immediately or permanently, but I am genuinely helped. The presence of Scripture and thankfulness may not eradicate every anxious thought, but it introduces a new and good scaffolding in the landscape of my swirling mind, so that anxious thoughts do not get to monopolize all the real estate.

God Gives True Peace

After talking about continual prayer and thanksgiving, Philippians 4:6–7 (ESV) continues with talking about the peace of God:

> Do not be anxious about anything, but in everything by prayer and supplication with thanksgiving let your requests be made known to God. And the peace of God, which surpasses all understanding, will guard your hearts and your minds in Christ Jesus.

I mentioned the Greek definition of "anxious" in Philippians 4:6 is the Greek word *merimnate*, which means to overly care about something or someone to the point of distraction.[20] To be divided. To go to pieces because you are being pulled in different directions. This is often our reality of living in a fallen world. However, the definition of peace in verse 7 is from the Greek word *eiréné*, which means rest and wholeness "*when all essential parts are joined together*."[21] In that sense, the verse could read this way: "And the uniting, restorative power of God to make what was divided whole again will guard your hearts and your minds in Christ Jesus." Peace is not the absence of pain, angst, or affliction. Peace is God's gift of wholeness amid being called to suffer pain, angst, and affliction. When we come to God divided in heart, casting our cares onto Him, asking Him for what we need, and thanking Him for all the ways He's already ministering to us, we somehow walk away whole.

I'm sure this has happened to you after a long session of prayer. It's not like the problem itself immediately went away, and it's not like you'll never get anxious again, but for that moment, the transfer of trust went from you to God, and you felt the release. You were divided, pulled in a million directions, and then, after coming into the presence of God, you were united, joined together again, and offered a singular, upward focus: the Lord. He lifted your chin, took your burden, and stitched you back together. When you walk out of that exchange, earthly concerns may still linger, but you don't fear them nearly as much. How could you, when you just encountered the most restorative power in the world? Perhaps this is what the psalmist is getting at when he asks God to "unite my heart to fear your name."[22] The Lord can help you counter the catastrophizing thoughts with truth. Paul ends his thought saying,

---

20. Strong's Lexicon, s.v. "be anxious for," https://biblehub.com/strongs/philippians/4-6.htm.
21. Strong's Lexicon, s.v. 1515 "eiréné," https://biblehub.com/greek/1515.htm, emphasis added.
22. Psalm 86:11 ESV

> Finally, brothers, whatever is true, whatever is honorable, whatever is just, whatever is pure, whatever is lovely, whatever is commendable, if there is any excellence, if there is anything worthy of praise, think about these things.[23]

To counter negative self-talk, seek out the truth. One way is to ask ourselves questions like, "What are the odds of this happening or being true?" "I have my ideas about what the outcome will be, is it possible I could be wrong?" "If the thing I greatly fear happens, how bad would it be and how will I cope?" "What does God's Word say about it?"

In his book *A Quest for Godliness*, J. I. Packer says, "The healthy Christian . . . [is one] who has a sense of God's presence stamped deep on his soul, who trembles at God's word, who lets it dwell in him richly by constant meditation upon it, and who tests and reforms his life daily in response to it."[24] As we cling to God's Word amid a world that is used to exchanging lies, we wage war against the temptation to take up our cares ourselves. Instead, we can meditate upon that which is true and take our cares to the One who is true since He is able to help us.

The old saints used to sing, "This peace that I have, the world didn't give it, the world can't take it away." And they told the truth. The passage says "the peace *of God.*" This unifying, restorative peace is *God's* to give, and He has chosen to give it to us through Christ. And as we seek Him with our calamities, woes, and worries—thanking Him for His grace where it is found—He fills us with more of His peace. No one can take away what God chooses to give. So let us run to it repeatedly.

---

23. Philippians. 4:8 ESV
24. J. I. Packer, *A Quest for Godliness: The Puritan Vision for the Christian Life* (Crossway, 1994), 116.

CHAPTER 11

Made to Tremble

In the Chronicles of Narnia, when Susan and Lucy find Aslan dead on the stone table, they respond in anxiety and fear. But when Aslan surprises them by rising in resurrection glory, and they witness his great roar—a roar that even makes the trees tremble—they jump on his back and ride to join him in his work of bringing dead Narnians back to life. On the way, as they ride on the risen Aslan's back, Susan and Lucy feel a sensation they never had before—a sensation that sounds a lot like trembling, but in a good way:

> [The] next moment the whole world seemed to turn upside down, and the children felt as if they had left their insides behind them; for the Lion had gathered himself together for a greater leap than any he had yet made and jumped—or you may call it flying rather than jumping—right over the castle wall. The two girls, breathless but unhurt, found themselves tumbling off his back in the middle of a wide stone courtyard full of statues.[1]

Feeling as if our insides were left behind us somewhere. Not just jumping but flying over castle walls. *Breathless but unhurt.* This is exactly what it means to tremble the right way for Susan and Lucy. And as it turns out, the same is true for us.

---

1. C. S. Lewis, *The Lion, the Witch, and the Wardrobe* (1950; repr., HarperCollins, 2002), 182.

We have been made to tremble, but anxiety is not our primary identity. Our primary identity is that we stand in awe of the One who we primarily tremble before. Our friend Flavel once again helps us consider religious fear. He defines it as "the awful filial fear of God."[2] It is not a terror because we are concerned about condemnation, for that type of fear has to do with punishment, and our punishment has been placed on Christ.[3] This is a sanctified fear, an awe and reverence inspired by love and respect as a child to his or her father.

In Exodus 2, the story of Moses teaches us about this. If you remember Moses's origin story, he was placed in a basket that floated down the Nile when he was a baby. The name Moses means "drawn out from the water."[4] In the Hebrew mind, water (and especially the sea or unpredictable rivers) was associated with turmoil, chaos, and death. The Nile River was a place of distress since male infants were being drowned in the water in accordance with Pharoah's order. So why would a mother in this context place a baby in a basket floating down a river? His mother places him in a basket in the river, not to destroy his life, but to save it. She names him according to her hope—he is drawn out of that water, rescued by God's mercy from this river of death.

Time passes and Moses grows up. Eventually, we find him on the run from Pharaoh for killing an Egyptian. He flees to Midian and meets the seven daughters of a priest near a well. We see Moses's strength in how he defends these women from other shepherds.[5] He is welcomed into this priest's family and begins living in this foreign land. Fast-forward to Exodus 3, and Moses is doing the ordinary work of shepherding his father-in-law's flock near Mount Sinai. It is here when a miraculous revelation comes to Moses: God reveals Himself through an angel of the Lord. This angel appears to Moses in a bush that is blazing with fire but not consumed. As Moses examines this

---

2. John Flavel, "A Practical Treatise of Fear" in *The Whole Works of John Flavel*, Vol. 3 (London: W. Baynes and Son, 1820), 244.
3. 1 John 4:18
4. Exodus 2:10
5. Exodus 2:17

miracle, God calls out to him, "Moses, Moses! . . . I am the God of your father, the God of Abraham, the God of Isaac, and the God of Jacob." And here's how the rest of the encounter unfolded:

> Moses hid his face because he was afraid to look at God. [Remind you of anyone?] Then the LORD said, "I have observed the misery of my people in Egypt, and have heard them crying out because of their oppressors. I know about their sufferings, and I have come down to rescue them from the power of the Egyptians and to bring them from that land to a good and spacious land, a land flowing with milk and honey—the territory of the Canaanites, Hethites, Amorites, Perizzites, Hivites, and Jebusites. So because the Israelites' cry for help has come to me, and I have also seen the way the Egyptians are oppressing them, therefore, go. I am sending you to Pharaoh so that you may lead my people, the Israelites, out of Egypt." But Moses asked God, "Who am I that I should go to Pharaoh and that I should bring the Israelites out of Egypt?"[6]

That last line says so much. At this point, Moses didn't have confidence in himself. He said, "Who am I that I should go . . . ?" Moses was not placing his confidence in his ability. Toward God, he was afraid to even look. For his people, he was afraid to even speak. He was no longer the strong Moses who previously defended others in Midian, fought the Egyptian who struck the Hebrew,[7] or dissuaded the shepherds from driving the women away.[8] Years had passed since then, and Moses now recognized his weakness. In the face of an uncontrollable and daunting situation, Moses had a choice on where to run for safety. So where *did* he find safety? His fears were eclipsed by what God revealed about Himself.

6. Exodus 3:4, 6–11
7. Exodus 2:11–12
8. Exodus 2:17–19

> He answered, "I will certainly be with you, and this will be the sign to you that I am the one who sent you: when you bring the people out of Egypt, you will all worship God at this mountain. Then Moses asked God, "If I go to the Israelites and say to them, 'The God of your ancestors has sent me to you,' and they ask me, 'What is his name?' what should I tell them?" God replied to Moses, "I AM WHO I AM. This is what you are to say to the Israelites: I AM has sent me to you." God also said to Moses, "Say this to the Israelites: The LORD, the God of your ancestors, the God of Abraham, the God of Isaac, and the God of Jacob, has sent me to you. This is my name forever; this is how I am to be remembered in every generation.[9]

God revealed His name to Moses, when He said, "I AM WHO I AM." I AM WHO I AM is the English translation of the Hebrew "Ehyeh asher Ehyeh,"[10] which is the first person of the verb "to be." In other words, God will always be who He is. He is self-existent, self-sufficient, eternal, and unchangeable. God exists on His own, is sustained by His own power, upholds His own will, and never loses His ability to be Himself. He is always the same from age to age, never bound by time, place, or circumstance. He exists outside of any material or physical bounds, yet He is ever-present, all-knowing, and all-powerful. *This is why He is indeed a safe place.* Nothing causes the character of the Alpha and Omega to flip or make an alteration. There is good news for the anxious, and it is this: God is never found trembling. The Great I AM is stable, steady, and safe.

By choosing to fear God—Moses was able to lead God's people through the uncontrollable and the impossible. God used a man who was afraid to speak to accomplish His will. The purpose of God for

---

9. Exodus 3:12–15
10. Bethany Verrett, "Why Does God Call Himself 'I Am Who I Am'?" Bible Study Tools, February 22, 2023, https://www.biblestudytools.com/bible-study/topical-studies/why-does-god-call-himself-i-am-that-i-am.html.

Moses was that he was drawn out from the waters of distress so that he might help deliver others from the waters of distress—not through his own strength but through God's power.

A Holy Fear

There is a kind of fear we were made for, whether we are currently anxious or not, and that's holy fear (or what Flavel called religious fear). Scripture tells us that we are to fear the Lord. This fear for Christians is not a response based on pending judgment for unrepentant sins; that type of fear has been driven out by God's love.[11] Nor is it what we cling to in order to guarantee we will get rid of our anxious fears as some books suggest. What does fear of the Lord look like? What does this type of trembling before God look like? It looks like the kind of fear Susan and Lucy experienced—a fear that leaves us breathless but unhurt. Captivated, amazed, to the point that our insides drop and we tremble in awe. Or, if Narnia isn't your cup of coffee and you'd rather explore a biblical example, let's consider Moses at Mount Sinai.

When Moses ascended Mount Sinai in Exodus 19–20, he did so on behalf of God's people. They were finally free from Egyptian slavery and ready to become their own new nation. They are all gathered at the base of the mountain and Moses ascends as a mediator between them and God. As Moses meets with God, God speaks to him about the covenant He will make with them and how on the third day He will come down before the people. While Moses is still on the mountain, the people were brought to the base of Mount Sinai to watch and to wait. To prove the exchange between God and Moses was legitimate, God said to Moses: "I am going to come to you in a dense cloud, so that the people will hear when I speak with you and will always believe you."[12]

God didn't just promise that His presence would come to Sinai; He also promised there was a certain way to encounter His presence.

11. 1 John 4:18
12. Exodus 19:9

In order to witness this grand event at the foot of the mountain, the people must be consecrated by washing their clothes, and they must stay inside certain boundaries that are set around the mountain: "Put boundaries for the people all around the mountain and say: Be careful that you don't go up on the mountain or touch its base. Anyone who touches the mountain must be put to death. No hand may touch him; instead, he will be stoned or shot with arrows and not live, whether animal or human. When the ram's horn sounds a long blast, they may go up the mountain."[13] They had a clean enough covering to come somewhat near the Lord's presence, but not a strong enough covering to enter it. The time came.

> On the morning of the third day there were thunders and lightnings and a thick cloud on the mountain and a very loud trumpet blast, so that ***all the people in the camp trembled.*** Then Moses brought the people out of the camp to meet God, and they took their stand at the foot of the mountain. Now Mount Sinai was wrapped in smoke because the LORD had descended on it in fire. The smoke of it went up like the smoke of a kiln, and the ***whole mountain trembled*** greatly. And as the sound of the trumpet grew louder and louder, Moses spoke, and God answered him in thunder. The LORD came down on Mount Sinai, to the top of the mountain. And the LORD called Moses to the top of the mountain, and Moses went up. . . . All the people witnessed the thunder and lightning, the sound of the ram's horn, and the mountain surrounded by smoke. When the people saw it they ***trembled*** and stood at a distance. "You speak to us, and we will listen," they said to Moses, "but don't let God speak to us, or we will die."[14]

---

13. Exodus 19:12–13
14. Exodus 19:16–20 ESV, emphasis added; Exodus 20:18–19, emphasis added

Hebrews 12:21 says that the Israelites weren't the only ones trembling at this moment. So was their leader: "The appearance was so terrifying that Moses said, I am trembling with fear."

The mountain, the people, and Moses all have the same response to this intense display of God's thunderous presence and power: trembling. In fact, even demons respond this way to the one true God.[15] And understandably so! Who *wouldn't* respond this way? The Israelites were facing pending judgment for unrepentant sins. They were in a vulnerable and terrifying position. Israel would die if they crossed the boundary into God's presence. And yet here's the wild part: you won't.

How can this be? We learned back in chapter 5 that you're completely covered in Christ's righteousness—which reorients our relationship with God based upon the identity of Jesus Christ bringing a perfect atonement and security which leads us to awe. This means you now have unfiltered access to the I AM, not through Moses, but through the greater Prophet and Mediator: Jesus. When Moses was the mediator, God gave the law to anxious Israel and they worshipped an idol.[16] Now, with Jesus as our Mediator, God gives us anxious saints His Word and fills us with His Spirit that we may worship Him in reverence. Not only did Jesus uphold the law that was given to Moses, but He provided through His own body the singular satisfactory means of atonement through His own blood, showing Himself to be both a better sacrifice than animals could ever be and a better Priest and Mediator than any mere human could be. Being that He is divine, He was holy and had direct access to the Father. Being that He was human, He could experience our temptations and prevail, "being obedient to the point of death,"[17]—even stretching out His body on the cross as He wore the crown of thorns, He displayed Himself the better King. This King of kings resurrected from the dead, evidencing that God the Father approved and confirmed His Son's ability to

15. James 2:19
16. Exodus 32
17. Philippians 2:8

save a people for Himself.[18] This King is our mercy that triumphs over judgment.[19] As we have trusted in Jesus, we have found that by grace and through faith we receive a new identity with sanctified responsibilities.[20] It's God's amazing grace that makes the way for us being safe in our gospel identity with Christ, our better and greater Prophet, Priest, and King has secured for us.

This means that in Christ, you can cross the boundary into the holy. You can enter God's presence under the protection of Christ's blood and His righteous record. You can not only come *somewhat* near the Lion of Judah, but you can ride on His back all the way to glory. The veil that once blocked us from God's presence is torn. And that should leave you even more in awe than those at Sinai were. That should leave you trembling in a good way: breathless at the fact that you are unharmed. God solved the greatest problem in human history—the problem that humans are most anxious about, deep down. And if He solved that deepest problem, He is sure to be trusted with many more.

Falling Down in Prayer

Another way we were made to tremble is in the way we intercede for others. Consider Moses again. When he came down the mountain with God's Law, he observed the Israelites' stiff-necked idolatry as they turned away from Yahweh to worship a golden calf. Their irreverence and lack of amazement at the nature of God caused Moses to fall and tremble. Moses was afraid for them because they did not fear God. Their idolatry stirred the holy anger of God, who had just given the law to His prophet to instruct these wanderers in His ways. Moses fell down, shook, and began interceding for them. In his own words, he says:

> "So I went back down the mountain . . . I saw how you had sinned against the LORD your God; you had

18. Romans 4:25
19. James 2:13
20. Ephesians 2:8–10

> made a calf image for yourselves. You had quickly turned from the way the LORD had commanded for you. . . . I fell down like the first time in the presence of the LORD for forty days and forty nights; I did not eat food or drink water because of all the sin you committed, doing what was evil in the LORD's sight and angering him. . . . [Y]ou rebelled against the command of the LORD your God. You did not believe or obey him. You have been rebelling against the LORD ever since I have known you. I fell down in the presence of the LORD forty days and forty nights because the LORD had threatened to destroy you. I prayed to the LORD: 'Lord GOD, do not annihilate your people, your inheritance, whom you redeemed through your greatness and brought out of Egypt with a strong hand. Remember your servants Abraham, Isaac, and Jacob. Disregard this people's stubbornness, and their wickedness and sin.'"[21]

When our mind is free from the fretfulness that comes with wondering about our deepest problem, our attention naturally turns to others who have not experienced the relief in Christ that we have. Moses's example is one for us all. Do we respond this way when we see loved ones rebelling against God? Do we fall, trembling at the thought of our loved ones not knowing the Lord? Do we lay prostrate to intercede for them?

We can take our deep, gut-level concerns for our neighbors to God. This is a holy sort of fear, one that not just Moses knew in relation to Israel, but Paul knew too, in relation to Gentiles: "While Paul was waiting for them in Athens, he was deeply distressed when he saw that the city was full of idols,"[22] Jesus, too, knew what it was to look out over a city in need of repentance, and weep for it.[23] There are a

21. Deuteronomy 9:15–18, 23–27
22. Acts 17:16
23. Matthew 23:37; Luke 19:41

million ways we should not shutter or back down in this life. But to look upon our neighbors who are far from God and tremble in intercession for them is exactly the posture we should take. Why? Because rejecting God's Word spoken through His prophets shook the earth in the Old Testament, and Scripture says that rejecting Christ Jesus now shakes the earth and the heavens. This was experienced through Moses, as we've already seen, but also through the prophet Haggai when the Lord declared:

> "This is the promise I made to you when you came out of Egypt, and my Spirit is present among you; don't be afraid." The LORD of Armies says this: "Once more, in a little while, I am going to shake the heavens and the earth, the sea, and the dry land. I will shake all the nations so that the treasures of all the nations will come, and I will fill this house with glory," says the LORD of Armies. "The silver and gold belong to me"—this is the declaration of the LORD of Armies. "The final glory of this house will be greater than the first," says the LORD of Armies. "I will provide peace in this place"—this is the declaration of the LORD of Armies."[24]

The writer of Hebrews in 12:25–29 explains this text by saying:

> See to it that you do not reject the one who speaks. For if they did not escape when they rejected him who warned them on earth, even less will we if we turn away from him who warns us from heaven. His voice shook the earth at that time, but now he has promised, **Yet once more I will shake not only the earth but also the heavens.** This expression, "Yet once more," indicates the removal of what can be shaken—that is, created things—so that what is not shaken might remain. Therefore, since we are

24. Haggai 2:5–9

> receiving a kingdom that cannot be shaken, let us be thankful. By it, we may serve God acceptably, with reverence and awe, for our God is a consuming fire.

Do you see how this passage speaks to those in Christ and those outside of it? For those outside of Christ, it is a warning: There is no escaping the consequences that come with rejecting Him. God will shake and destroy whatever the unbeliever hopes in outside of Christ, taking the unbeliever down with it. Their false idols will tremble, break apart, and fall. And so will they. Or as Job puts it: "God is wise and all-powerful. Who has opposed him and come out unharmed? . . . He shakes the earth from its place so that its pillars tremble."[25] On the flip side, do you also see that it says God will shake everything from its place so those things that cannot be shaken will remain?

One day, God will shake everything to expose His kingdom that cannot be shaken. Because we have this unshaken kingdom now, we stand in holy fear—in "reverence and awe"—of our God. We stand amazed that in all this shaking, under the protection of Christ, we'd somehow remain unharmed. And at the same time, we pray and knock and beg for those who are not under that protection yet. Like Moses, we who have no reason to be anxious for the future can throw all our labors into interceding for those who do.

The Weightiness of God

Along with falling down in intercession, there is a third way our fear of the Lord might manifest itself in our bodies, and that's found in Deuteronomy 10:12. This passage tells us that fearing the Lord is the essence of knowing Him, walking with Him, loving Him, and worshipping Him.

> "And now, Israel, what does the LORD your God ask of you except to ***fear the LORD your God*** by walking in all his ways, to love him, and to worship the LORD

25. Job 9:4, 6

> your God with all your heart and all your soul?" (emphasis added)

When we've been captivated by God's majesty, we respond in the fear of the Lord by loving Him and worshipping Him with all that we have, which is naturally manifested in not just soul but body. We *walk* in all His ways.

Seeing the fear of the Lord defined this way reveals that the fear of God is simply assigning Him the weight He deserves in our life. The question is this then: To what do you assign the most weight in *your* life? That will tell you what you most "fear" in life apart from the Lord. If you aren't sure of the answer, just look at what you love and worship—and whose ways you walk in. What do you offer your body in service to? The answer will tell you what truly makes you tremble. For example,

- If money is the weightiest matter in your life, the majority of your days (and mental energy) will be spent walking in the instructions of your financial advisor. You might desire to follow Jesus's instructions about money, but often you gloss over those commands in order to prioritize wealth. Which means at the end of the day, you fear money more than God.
- If beauty is the weightiest matter in your life, you spend the majority of your time finding the latest beauty products, clothes, and filters to try to preserve your looks and how you present to others. You neglect the Lord's call toward inner beauty. This is fearing aging, prioritizing vanity, and idolizing youthfulness over God.
- If family is the weightiest matter in your life, you spend the majority of your time guarding time with your biological family, and not showing hospitality to church family and neighbors, whether

believing or unbelieving. You fear family and their disappointment more than God.

- If admiration or reputation is the weightiest matter in your life, you spend the majority of your time focused upon how you think others perceive you. Often paralyzed by wanting to please and not disappoint, you place man and their opinion in the place of God. This is fearing man more than God.
- If power is the weightiest matter in your life, you will lie, steal, and kill to get it, justifying how it is God's will for you, even if injustice and ungodliness is the way you attain it. You fear power more than God.
- If approval is the weightiest matter in your life, then you will close your mouth when you should speak out and speak out when you should be silent because you believe this is what that person who you want to keep in your favor thinks and you don't want to disappoint them. So even if it means ignoring the voice of God and disobeying Him, you will because you fear man's approval more than God.

This does not mean that we have no concerns in this life or that when we tremble before God, we no longer tremble because of anything else. We experience many fears and trials in this life, and God wants us to bring these burdens to Him. As Christians, Scripture tells us the truth: Our fear of God should be greater than our sinful anxieties. When we get it the other way around, we find ourselves trembling before the wrong god.

Believers tremble before God because we have assigned Him the most weight in our lives. We acknowledge His power and holy glory, which are higher than any earthly powers we may fear. By His grace, we have not turned away from Him to idols, and if we have, we are able to go to Him in repentance. We daily turn toward Him and tremble before Him because only His kingdom cannot be shaken. We are in awe of God, more poignantly than sinful and "frightful giants" we are tempted to fear. We are not scared of Him but humbly devoted to Him because we recognize His hallowed grandeur. We hear and obey Jesus when He says,

> "I say to you, my friends, don't fear those who kill the body and, after that can do nothing more. But I will show you the one to fear: Fear him who has authority to throw people into hell after death. Yes, I say to you, this is the one to fear!"[26]

Anchored in Our Gospel Identity and Spiritual Family

Did you know God wants you to be certain about the fact that you're safe in Him? Did you know He wants you to be certain about your identity in Him—that *you're His child forever*, and nothing can ever threaten to take you out of His family and His fatherly care? Some think that being this secure in who God says we are is a form of pride, but the book of Hebrews calls it "strong encouragement," which allows us to "seize the hope before us." Here's the full passage:

> For when God made a promise to Abraham, since he had no one greater to swear by, he swore by himself: "I will indeed bless you, and I will greatly multiply you." And so, after waiting patiently, Abraham obtained the promise. For people swear by something greater than themselves, and for them a confirming oath ends every dispute. Because God wanted to show his ***unchangeable purpose*** even more clearly to the heirs of the promise, he guaranteed it with an oath, so that through two unchangeable things, in which it is impossible for God to lie, ***we who have fled for***

26. Luke 12:4–5

> ***refuge might have strong encouragement to seize the hope set before us. We have this hope as an anchor for the soul, firm and secure.*** It enters the inner sanctuary behind the curtain. Jesus has entered there on our behalf as a forerunner.[27]

God made a covenant with Abraham that he would be the "father of many nations." This meant that his line would be the means of ushering in the Messiah. The writer of Hebrews reminds us in this passage that God promised Abraham He'd create a worldwide family through Abraham's line. And He kept that promise. This is why it says, "Now the promises were spoken to Abraham and to his seed. He does not say 'and to seeds,' as though referring to many, but referring to one, ***and to your seed***, who is Christ."[28] God fulfilling His promise to Abraham is referred to as His "unchangeable purpose." Nothing will hold God back from fulfilling His plan to redeem people from all parts of the world through Christ. He will not change His mind; the Father is going to keep multiplying His people across the earth, bringing them into His great family. The fulfillment of that promise started with the birth of Isaac, Abraham's son, and ended in Christ, who brought not just believing Jews into His promise, but even Gentiles, since the qualification for coming is not heritage but faith. In this passage, God swears by His own name and by oath that He will keep this promise.

Why would He need to do this? Because in the time this passage was written, Christians were trembling from persecution and hostility. In their affliction, they wondered if God's promise about their place in His worldwide family was still true. From their vantage point, it didn't look like they were multiplying; it looked like they were being stamped out. They were facing storm after storm. It is precisely in this kind of trembling that God wanted to *double*-ensure they knew His plan was still in motion and that they were safe in their identity as His people. He was going to honor His promises and His covenants to His children. He wanted them to experience a deep confidence that they

---

27. Hebrews 6:13–20a, emphasis added
28. Galatians 3:16, emphasis added

were indeed part of God's great family—a family that would not just multiply throughout the world, but one day overcome the world and reign with His Messiah. It may not seem safe in their current moment to be a Christian, but in the end, He wanted them to know that being in God's family will eventually be the safest place on the planet.

In Christ, we're brought into this great family. We are "heirs of the promise" which means we are "heirs of God" and "coheirs with Christ."[29] This means that when circumstances don't *seem* safe and we tremble in our own storms, God wants us to flee into Him, our vessel of love. We can be encouraged that we belong to Him, seize the hope we have in our future, and feel anchored and secure about the end of our story.

An anchor is a metal device that secures a vessel to the bed of a body of water to keep it from drifting. Our hope secures us to God and His promises to keep us from drifting because of life's difficulties. I love how it says that those of us who have fled for refuge are able to have this firm, secure hope based upon the unchangeable character of God. This hope anchors or controls our soul even if in our anxiety we feel that we are untethered to it. This covenant God makes with us via His oath is coming from the One who does not lie. He cannot lie,[30] because He is the Truth.[31] The writer bases all of these comforting truths—which are realized in Christ in our lives—on the character of God. This truth has brought great comfort in times of overwhelming distress.

We must grapple with the fact that there is no place in this world where we are safe except in the arms of our Father. There are thousands of possibilities of things going wrong. We look out and see a dangerous sea. We look up and see the dark, brimming clouds above. So, what are we to do? Do we spend our time rolling all those possibilities over in our minds again and again? Or do we seize the hope that is ours? Do we lean into the strong encouragement God wants to give us, believing God's oath that He will keep the many promises He makes

29. Hebrews 6:17; Romans 8:17
30. Numbers 23:19; Titus 1:2; Hebrews 6:18
31. John 1:14–17; 14:6; 1 John 5:20

to His children until the end? In their trembling times, the readers of Hebrews had to answer these questions. In the end, they were told to fear God, banking on *His* character to drive His family safely through the storm, all the way to the end. In our trembling times, we're encouraged toward the same.

Why? Because We Have a Glorious Future

There is a fourth good reason for a Christian to tremble, and it is at the sight of our glorious future. In John 11, Mary and Martha sent a word to Jesus about their brother, Lazarus. Here's what they said, and here's how Jesus responds:

> So the sisters sent a message to [Jesus]: "Lord, the one you love is sick." When Jesus heard it, he said, "This sickness will not end in death but is for the glory of God, so that the Son of God may be glorified through it." Now Jesus loved Martha, her sister, and Lazarus. So when he heard that he was sick, he stayed two more days in the place where he was.[32]

The way this story unfolds is not at all what we would expect. Lazarus is sick to the point of dying. Jesus finds out about it, and did you see what he does in the passage? He doesn't leave right away to heal Lazarus. He decides to stay *two more days* where he was.[33] After those two days, Jesus tells the disciples that their friend Lazarus has fallen asleep (meaning he died).[34] Jesus said Lazarus's sickness wouldn't *end* in death, but that doesn't mean Lazarus didn't suffer to the point of death. Lazarus died. When Jesus finally arrives, Lazarus has been in the grave four days. Jesus loves them and could've healed Lazarus from a distance with a word, but He had a different plan. He waited. He allowed the sickness. He allowed the death. He chose to come in person to be with them and rescue them from the sting of death. These

32. John 11:3–6
33. John 11:6
34. John 11:11–14

sisters had been grieving with tears streaming for four days.[35] Jews had come to comfort them in their grief over those four days. Jesus knew these sisters were filled with grief and wept with them. Jesus knew that He would wake him up from death so all would be certain this was a resurrection not a resuscitation. But Lazarus and his sisters had to wait. Jesus's plan was much grander than theirs because He was preparing them for future glory.

> Then Martha said to Jesus, "Lord, if you had been here, my brother wouldn't have died. Yet even now I know that whatever you ask from God, God will give you."
>
> "Your brother will rise again," Jesus told her.

Jesus shines the light of hope on what seemed like a sealed grave.

> Martha said to him, "I know that he will rise again in the resurrection at the last day."
>
> Jesus said to her, "I am the resurrection and the life. The one who believes in me, even if he dies, will live. Everyone who lives and believes in me will never die. Do you believe this?"
>
> "Yes, Lord," she told him, "I believe you are the Messiah, the Son of God, who comes into the world."[36]

A few verses later, Jesus tells Martha, "Didn't I tell you that if you believed you would see the glory of God?"[37] Jesus calls life into Lazarus's body in the present as a way to point them all to the life awaiting—to their future glory. This was all about glory. Jesus used this instance to help them understand that for us Christians, while life may include sickness and falling asleep, there is a future glory that we are waiting for.

---

35. John 11:17
36. John 11:21–27
37. John 11:40

> After he said this, he shouted with a loud voice, "Lazarus, come out!" The dead man came out bound hand and foot with linen strips and with his face wrapped in a cloth. Jesus said to them, "Unwrap him and let him go."[38]

Can you imagine being in the crowd when the once-dead Lazarus strides out of the grave? A breathless, amazed, trembling wonder must have spread through the gathering of mourners. As for Mary, this would not be the last time she had to catch her breath after witnessing a once-dead man walking. Lazarus's resurrection was incredible in its own right, but it pointed forward to another, better resurrection—Christ's. She was granted a gift to take in the risen Christ with her own eyes.[39] And what was her response at witnessing her resurrected Savior? Along with a couple other women, "They went out and fled from the tomb, for trembling and astonishment had seized them."[40]

Trembling and astonishment. That's exactly what the Christian's response should be when we consider not only the reality of Christ's resurrection, but the fact that His resurrection into glory guarantees our own. His rising ensures that we will rise one day into a resurrected, regenerated future. This reminds us of 1 Thessalonians 4:16–18:

> For the Lord himself will descend from heaven with a shout, with the archangel's voice, and with the trumpet of God, and the dead in Christ will rise first. Then we who are still alive, who are left, will be caught up together with them in the clouds to meet the Lord in the air, and so we will always be with the Lord. Therefore encourage one another with these words.

The believer's hope causes us to look ahead and see the prophesies unfold. We will tremble at our master's voice as He ushers us into His

38. John 11:41–44
39. John 20:14–18
40. Mark 16:8 ESV

resurrection life, our future glory. To shake in holy amazement, as Mary did, is the only reasonable reaction to such a reality.

In conclusion, there are times when trembling isn't what we were made for. But there are other times when trembling is *exactly* what we were made for. By way of summary, let's take in the four ways we were made to tremble one more time:

1. When we consider the thundering God of the heavens and think of the distance Israel had to stand from Him so that they might not die, we should shudder in amazement that we can walk right up to God without an ounce of fear. We were made to tremble and rejoice at this access we now have to the Father through Christ, His Word. Against all odds, we can say confidently with the psalmist: "Sustain me as you have promised, and I will live . . . I tremble in awe of you."[41]
2. When we consider our loved ones who do not have this kind of access to God, we should buckle at the knees and fall down like Moses, interceding for them. It is right to pray that God might open the eyes of those whose current hopes will be shaken when God shakes the earth. As we approach our lost friends, we were made to say with Paul, "I came to you in weakness with great fear and trembling . . . not with wise and persuasive words, but with a demonstration of the Spirit's power, so that your faith might not rest on human wisdom, but on God's power."[42]
3. When we consider what a relationship with God really means, we should fear Him in the biblical sense. We were made to fear Him by loving Him, worshipping Him, and walking in His ways.

41. Psalm 119:116 NASB, 120
42. 1 Corinthians 2:3–5 NIV

God says we were made to be "those who are humble and contrite in spirit, and who tremble at my word," for "these are the ones I look on with favor."[43]

4. And finally, when we consider our glorious future in the resurrection, we should shiver with excitement, believing in God's promise that when that day finally comes, "the Lord himself will descend from heaven with a shout, with the archangel's voice, and with the trumpet of God, and the dead in Christ will rise first. Then we who are still alive, who are left, will be caught up together with them in the clouds to meet the Lord in the air, and so we will always be with the Lord."[44]

We were made to tremble before the One who never trembles. In our trembling we may be breathless, but we are ultimately unhurt.

---

43. Isaiah 66:2–3 NIV
44. 1 Thessalonians 4:16–17

CHAPTER 12

Do It Scared

Have you heard the phrase, "Do it scared?"[1] It means that we can take action, walk in God's will or calling for this season of our life, and be courageous in that calling despite feeling fear. The Bible has exhortations like "Be strong and courageous"[2] or "Be strong in the Lord"[3] or "The righteous are as bold as a lion."[4] How do we get there? In chapter 3, I mentioned the long list of saints who were afraid. We've considered some of those specific stories like Moses's call to lead and mediate for the Israelites, David's betrayal and persecution, and Paul's thorn in his flesh along with his constant awareness of his own weakness and trembling. How does one go from experiencing those types of fear to "doing it scared"? They live their lives unto God despite their fear.

All the biblical examples mentioned in this book are wonderful places to go for inspiration on doing it scared, but I want to consider a saint who existed outside of the pages of Scripture and yet his life proved to be an example of one living a life in accordance to Scripture despite a difficult trial.

In *My Bondage and My Freedom*, Frederick Douglass described how, as a teenager in 1833, his master committed him to Edward Covey's mastery for a year. Covey was known for breaking the will of the enslaved. Douglass secretly gave Mr. Covey the nickname "the snake" because of his cunning nature and the deceptions he used

---

1. Attributed to author and speaker Ruth Soukup, https://doitscared.com/.
2. Joshua 1:6–7, 9; Daniel 10:19; 1 Chronicles 28:20
3. Ephesians 6:10
4. Proverbs 28:1

to instill fear in the enslaved. Douglass reflected, "I was somewhat unmanageable when I first went there; but a few months of this discipline tamed me. Mr. Covey succeeded in breaking me. I was broken in body, soul, and spirit. My natural elasticity was crushed; my intellect languished; the disposition to read departed; the cheerful spark that lingered about my eye died; the dark night of slavery closed in upon me; and behold a man transformed into a brute!"[5]

Douglass was the recipient of violence and brutality as Covey "the snake" left him transformed into someone unrecognizable—someone left to feel unlike himself, absent of his humanity, existing as a mere "brute" or animal. One day, Covey sneakily tried to tie Douglass up and whip him. It is here that Douglass finally decided to stand up for himself against this slave-breaker. They tussled for hours. To Covey's surprise, Douglass was able to control the situation until Covey eventually gave up the thought of whipping him at all. Douglass said in response to this, "Well, my dear reader, this battle with Mr. Covey,—undignified as it was . . . was the turning point in my *'life as a slave.'* It rekindled in my breast the smouldering embers of liberty; it brought up my Baltimore dreams, and revived a sense of my own manhood. I was a changed being after that fight. I was *nothing* before: I WAS A MAN NOW." He then said, "I was no longer a servile coward, trembling under the frown of a brother worm dust, but my long-cowed spirit was roused to an attitude of manly independence. I had reached the point, at which *I was not afraid to die.* This spirit made me a freeman in *fact,* while I remained a slave in *form.*"[6]

For Douglass, it appears that remembering who he was—a man, made in the image of God, equal to Covey with every right to be free—gave him the power to experience liberty in the mind first, which in turn liberated his body. This moment in Douglas's story changed everything. His choice to "do it scared" was the catalyst to him fulfilling his dreams of freedom.

5. Frederick Douglass, *My Bondage and My Freedom* (1855; repr. Penguin Books, 2003), 160.
6. Douglass, *My Bondage and My Freedom*, 180–81, emphasis in original.

This harsh mastery reminds me of an even harsher one; when

The deceiver projects fiery darts and lie—

In wait to conceal Divine bounty.

Cause freedmen to forget due to constant lies.

Truth which loosens the tie that bind thee.

Our Savior Tempted

Before we consider how we might be tempted, let's look at our Savior who is tempted by the enemy for forty days in Matthew 4:1–11.

> Then Jesus was led up by the Spirit into the wilderness to be tempted by the devil. After he had fasted forty days and forty nights, he was hungry. Then the tempter approached him and said, "If you are the Son of God, tell these stones to become bread."
>
> He answered, "It is written: **Man must not live on bread alone but on every word that comes from the mouth of God**."
>
> Then the devil took him to the holy city, had him stand on the pinnacle of the temple, and said to him, "If you are the Son of God, throw yourself down. For it is written:
>
> > **He will give his angels orders concerning you,**
> > and **they will support you with their hands**
> > **so that you will not strike**
> > **your foot against a stone.**"
>
> Jesus told him, "It is also written: **Do not test the Lord your God**."
>
> Again, the devil took him to a very high mountain and showed him all the kingdoms of the world and their splendor. And he said to him, "I will give

> you all these things if you will fall down and worship me."
>
> Then Jesus told him, "Go away, Satan! For it is written: **Worship the Lord your God, and serve only him**."
>
> Then the devil left him, and angels came and began to serve him.

Jesus had been fasting, which meant that physically He would've been in a vulnerable state. Yet, when He was tempted, He conquered. The enemy tempted Him in three different ways: to sin through the lust of the flesh,[7] pride of life,[8] and the lust of the eyes.[9]

Yet despite all these temptations, our Savior perfectly upheld the law and obeyed God. Hebrews 2:17–18 says,

> He had to be like his brothers and sisters in every way, so that he could become a merciful and faithful high priest in matters pertaining to God, to make atonement for the sins of the people. For since he himself has suffered when he was tempted, he is able to help those who are tempted.

Spiritual Warfare

Our Lord's human nature allows Him to sympathize with us in our weaknesses. Seeing what our Lord experienced also reminds us that our situation is not merely physical but spiritual. When it comes to anxiety, we must never forget that we are not wrestling against flesh and blood; but we are facing spiritual forces of evil who wants to master us. Yet we have a God who "trains [our] hands for battle"[10]—not so that we fight in our own strength but so that we wage war in Christ

---

7. Matthew 4:3–4
8. Matthew 4:5–7
9. Matthew 4:8–10
10. Psalm 144:1

as His body. Ephesians 6:12 says, "For our struggle is not against flesh and blood, but against the rulers, against the authorities, against the cosmic powers of this darkness, against evil, spiritual forces in the heavens." Often, we are either unaware of these forces of evil or over-aware of them. Some Christians give their spiritual enemies no attention at all, and some Christians give the forces of darkness all their attention.

I recently spoke with a sister who was in tears because she feels anxiety rests on her like a burdensome yoke. She was exhausted from relentlessly being on the hunt for sin in her life, believing that because she is constantly anxious, God has abandoned her. She believed the lie that she had to fight this battle alone. That the responsibility to war against the comic forces was for her to carry. What saddened me was her community also told her if she is not winning the war, it is due to her lack of faith and inability to "rebuke the devil." Based upon how she was taught, her shield, protection, and power were bound up in her words.

Depending upon your theological background, you too might pray anxiously and often to "rebuke the devil" or pray all day against "the spirit of fear." This is exhausting and it's fighting anxiety with more anxiety. The Bible never tells Christians to rebuke the devil or his legions of demons. The Bible says Christians should *resist* the devil. James 4:7 says, "submit to God. Resist the devil, and he will flee from you." Similarly, 1 Peter 5:8–9 says,

> Be sober-minded, be alert. Your adversary the devil is prowling around like a roaring lion, looking for anyone he can devour. *Resist* him, firm in the faith, knowing that the same kind of sufferings are being experienced by your fellow believers throughout the world. (emphasis added)

"Doing it scared" is about resistance. We resist the devil by doing the opposite of what Adam and Eve did. Where they disobeyed God, we obey Him. They listened when the serpent said, "Did God really say?" But we listen when our Savior says, "Have you never read?"

When Jesus was tempted, He responded with "it is written." The serpent questions God's truth, but Jesus establishes the trustworthiness of God's truth. Through the Word we stand firm in our faith. The only person qualified to rebuke the devil is the Lord. Just look at these passages:

- "The LORD said to Satan, '*The* LORD rebuke you, Satan!'"[11]
- "Yet when Michael the archangel was disputing with the devil in an argument about Moses's body, he did not dare utter a slanderous condemnation against him but said, '*The Lord* rebuke you!'"[12]

Along with these passages, we must consider all the letters written to churches in the New Testament. Not one of them includes instructions on rebuking the devil. It's the Lord's job to rebuke the enemy. It's our job to resist him and stand firm in our faith. (If you are wondering what to do with passages that seem to grant Jesus's disciples authority over the enemy, consider this footnote.[13])

11. Zechariah 3:2, emphasis added
12. Jude 1:9, emphasis added
13. But what of passages like Luke 10:17–19, you might be asking. Yes, the *demons* submitted to the seventy-two disciples—not the devil himself. After all, Satan is not omnipresent and can only be at one place at a time. More than experiencing an attack by Satan, although it is possible, it is more likely that they were encountering his evil spiritual forces. And even then, the authority they were given over the enemy was not exercised in their own name. As they speak with Jesus about this, they say it is done "in *your* name." And on the other side of the ministry of the apostles throughout the book of Acts, we don't see any instructions to the established church regarding rebuking demons. If we scan through the New Testament letters to churches and pastors, there are plenty of commands about rebuking people (1 Tim. 5:1, 20; 2 Tim. 4:2; Titus 1:13; 2:15), but not one command about rebuking or exercising demons! If this practice was so central to a good relationship with God, why would zero churches be told to do this in the epistles? This doesn't mean that the enemy is no longer active and engaged in the work of destroying the faith of Christians. He is certainly just as active now as he was in the Gospels and the book of Acts. But the way the New Testament letters tell churches to resist the prowling enemy is through our union with Christ, resisting the devil, and righteous living.

So, if Scripture says resistance is not rebuking or chanting incantations against Satan, what *do* the New Testament letters teach when it comes to resisting Satan? They make it clear that one way to resist the devil is to just *keep obeying God*, even when the opposition is intense. Consider these passages:

- Keep forgiving when you'd rather be angry, and so overcome Satan's schemes to drive wedges between God's people (2 Cor. 2:7–11).
- Keep showing up to emotional and physical intimacy in your marriage, and so overcome Satan's temptations to distract you or tear down your self-control (1 Cor. 7:5).
- Keep running to the Lord's strength in thorns and trials to avoid Satan's temptation toward self-exaltation (2 Cor. 12:7).
- Keep showing up to God's people and Christian community, and so resist Satan's attempts at hindering you and isolating you (1 Thess. 2:17–20).
- Keep your pledges and promises. And also, if you're tempted to marry someone who believes in a false god, make the hard choice to walk away from the relationship that could draw you away from God, and stay faithful to your Christian faith. Doing this resists the heart-tugs that Satan uses to draw you away from God (1 Tim. 5:11–15).
- Keep telling the truth, and keep up the habit of resolving conflict and reconciling with brothers and sisters you are angry with. Doing this cuts off the enemy's opportunity to tempt you toward lying or burning with anger (Eph. 4:25–26).
- Keep giving instead of hoarding up your treasures, so that you don't fall into worshipping money, one of the snares of the devil (1 Tim. 6:9).

- Keep doing the right thing, especially when it comes to loving others, and so reveal that you are not a child of the devil, but a child of the Father (1 John 3:8–10).

Along with recognizing the enemy and living righteously, resistance requires putting on the right protective covering. Only a rash, conceited person jumps into an NFL-level brawl with no pads or helmet. But a person who *knows* they are weak? A person who *knows* their trembling arms and legs will get decimated out on the field without the right protective gear? That person has a real fighting chance, because rather than go out exposed and alone, they will cling to their protective covering.

We talked about the way God covers us in chapter 5. He overcame our deepest fears of exposure and separation from God. Do you remember how He did it? From top to bottom, our sin and shame is covered *in Christ.* And guess what? That's the exact same covering we need to resist the enemy. When it comes to remaining steadfast in the Lord's will and calling, the best way to "do it scared" is not through anxious rebuke but through being clothed in Christ. Ephesians 6:10–17 says:

> Finally, be strengthened by the Lord and by his vast strength. Put on the full armor of God so that you can stand against the schemes of the devil. For our struggle is not against flesh and blood, but against the rulers, against the authorities, against the cosmic powers of this darkness, against evil, spiritual forces in the heavens. For this reason take up the full armor of God, so that you may be able to resist in the evil day, and having prepared everything, to take your stand. Stand, therefore, with truth like a belt around your waist, righteousness like armor on your chest, and your feet sandaled with readiness for the gospel of peace. In every situation take up the shield of faith with which you can extinguish all the flaming arrows

> of the evil one. Take the helmet of salvation and the sword of the Spirit—which is the word of God.

The six pieces of armor listed in this passage all point back to Christ. Truthful, righteous, faithful, saving, overcoming the enemy with the Word, walking in this world to extend good news of peace with God—put together, these features are a picture of Jesus Himself. This panoply is what the body of Christ must be clothed in ultimately so that we might stand against the enemy. Christians wear the belt of Truth, the breastplate of Righteousness, feet readied with the gospel of Peace, the shield of Faith, the helmet of Salvation, and last (the only defensive weapon listed), the sword of the Spirit, which is the Word of God. Not only are these pieces of armor pointing to Christ, but many of them are also pieces of armor listed in the Old Testament as worn by God, our Divine Warrior.[14] The body of Christ must be covered or clothed in our God. It is the only way to resist the enemy, since our victory is in our union with Christ. I won't go into every piece of armor, but I want us to spend some time considering the shield of faith.

Shield of Faith

Notice the Scripture is expressed in an active voice. It says, "take up!" Don't just put on, take up. The shield was an important piece of defensive weaponry. Throughout the Old Testament, God often refers to Himself or is referred to as a Shield. This shield Paul is referring to would not have been a shield which is the size of a metal trash can lid, rather, this shield would have been large like the size of a door. This door-sized shield was often covered in leather and dipped in water to put out the enemy's fiery arrows. This faith is taking up a confident trust in God, which the church should have in every situation, at all times. When we have faith, we are able to extinguish the flaming arrows of the evil one.

Barnes in his commentary on Ephesians says, "By the 'fiery darts of the wicked,' Paul here refers, probably, to the temptations of the

14. Isaiah 59:17

great adversary, which are like fiery darts; or those furious suggestions of evil, and excitements to sin, which he may throw into the mind like fiery darts. They are blasphemous thoughts, unbelief, sudden temptation to do wrong, or thoughts that wound and torment the soul."[15] Paul is saying that Christ is more powerful than any adversary along with their demonic activity. Christ will keep us safe from evil powers. So, when . . .

- **The flaming arrows of doubt** come and we're wondering, "Lord, why do You feel so far away in this season?" . . .
- **The flaming arrows of having a child or family member who is a prodigal,** and you have been praying and you don't see any change yet . . .
- **The flaming arrows of anxiety and depression** seem to cripple you and you're wondering, "How long will I have to suffer, Lord, and hear those around me tell me to have more faith or to just trust the Lord?"
- **The flaming arrows of grief** which creep up on you when you least expect it . . .
- **The flaming arrows against your reputation** when vindication doesn't appear to be in sight . . .
- **The flaming arrows of persecution** if we are called to suffer for Christ . . .

. . . **we remember that Scripture says in Hebrews 11:1 (ESV): "Now faith is the assurance of things hoped for, the conviction of things not seen.**"

When we consider this passage in Hebrews, and we keep in mind from Ephesians that faith is to be our shield against the enemy (in tandem with all the other pieces of God's armor), what can we conclude? We can conclude that exercising faith is simply how the church hides

15. Albert Barnes, "Commentary on Ephesians 6," "Barnes' Notes on the Whole Bible," https://www.studylight.org/commentaries/eng/bnb/ephesians-6.html.

in God even when we have not yet seen the physical manifestation of our spiritual reality. This is how despite our doubts we can continue to ask God for the ability to reconcile our doubts and trust in Him even when we don't understand. This is how mothers, fathers, sisters, and brothers in Christ can keep praying for twenty or thirty years for one child or family member to know Christ personally. It's how when fear, anxiety, and depression are near, we can know no matter how we feel, God is with us in our suffering. It's knowing that He doesn't leave us alone in our grief. It's knowing that even if our reputation is soiled, what truly matters is who God says we are. It's, when faced with persecution, knowing the Beatitudes call us blessed and says that the kingdom of heaven is ours. It's walking with a confidence in God despite our present circumstance because we know the end of God's story—so we trust Him and continue to walk by faith and not by sight.

Our Lord is divine and able to protect us. When we put on His armor and hold up the shield of faith, we are given what we need to "do it scared."

Most comforting about God, though, is not just that He's divine and protective. In the person of Christ, He also knows what it's like to "do it scared." In other words, He doesn't simply command us to do something He's never had to do Himself. When the Son of God chose to leave heaven and take on flesh, He exposed Himself to the humility and terrors of humanity. The Suffering Servant laid aside His right to be served to serve us. He was resolved to wade into terrifying waters not only to expose Himself to temptation from His enemy, but to willingly[16] endure the cross appointed by His Father.[17] If we are looking for the Bible's quintessential example of what it means to do it scared—to exercise faith in a moment of deepest agony and trembling—we need only look to Christ in the garden of Gethsemane.

---

16. John 10:18
17. Acts 2:23

Our Lord in the Garden

As God, Jesus has sufficient resources; as a man, Jesus is completely dependent upon His Father. Before heading to the cross, the gospel of Luke tells us that:

> He went out and made his way as usual to the Mount of Olives, and the disciples followed him. When he reached the place, he told them, "Pray that you may not fall into temptation." Then he withdrew from them about a stone's throw, knelt down, and began to pray, "Father, if you are willing, take this cup away from me—nevertheless, not my will, but yours, be done."
>
> Then an angel from heaven appeared to him, strengthening him. Being in anguish, he prayed more fervently, and his sweat became like drops of blood falling to the ground. When he got up from prayer and came to the disciples, he found them sleeping, exhausted from their grief. "Why are you sleeping?" he asked them. "Get up and pray, so that you won't fall into temptation."[18]

Jesus's friends were not faithful and available; instead, they were found sleeping when their Lord asked them to watch and pray. When the Gospel of Luke describes this very scene, it says, "Being in anguish, he prayed more fervently, and his sweat became like drops of blood falling to the ground."[19] The word for agony here is *agónia*, which is used to describe a state of intense physical struggle that an athlete feels before an intense game and there is severe mental or emotional turmoil, fear, death, agony, and anxiety.[20]

Do you see how our greatest example of "do it scared" is Jesus? Consider what our Savior did when He was in agony. Did He give

---

18. Luke 22:39–46
19. Luke 22:44
20. Strong's Lexicon, s.v. 74 "*agónia*," https://biblehub.com/greek/74.htm.

up on the mission entirely? Did He bow out? No. He prayed more fervently and He asked His friends for help. His friends were found sleeping, but Jesus came back to approach them three times. Jesus continued to pray and not faint even when "his sweat became like drops of blood failing to the ground." As a doctor, the writer of Luke is describing a condition when one is under great anxiety. The sweating of blood is a rare medical condition showing that Jesus had been pushed to the extremes of His humanity. The National Library of Medicine describes this condition as "Hematohidrosis," saying it "is a very rare condition in which an individual sweats blood. It may occur in an individual who is suffering from extreme levels of stress."[21] Between Gethsemane and the cross, Jesus knew stress, weakness, angst, and deep sorrow. He knew what it was to come to grips with the most terrifying prospect in the world, and in response, He knew what it was to hide in His Father's wisdom, authority, and power for the strength He needed to endure. Again, I'll say it: Jesus, the God-man "did it scared." Yes, even Jesus experienced great agony, anxiety, and sorrow as He looked ahead to the cross awaiting Him.

We know how the story unfolds: Jesus set His face firmly on Calvary,[22] endured the cross with joy;[23] and He also faced anxieties. Even though He knew the Father would ultimately resurrect Him by the Spirit's power, He still had to consider the cost of pulling off heaven's redemption project. Knowing the end of the story did not change that fearful reality which caused Him to sweat drops of blood. Jesus shows us it is okay to have concerns. He had a natural concern for suffering and death. But He did not let His trial stop Him from running to His Father with His concerns or obeying God's will. Adam was in the garden anxious and hiding from his Father. Jesus, the Second Adam, is in the garden anxious yet praying to His Father. What are we doing in our garden?

---

21. Saugato Biswas et al., "A Curious Case of Sweating Blood," *Indian Journal of Dermatology* 58, no. 6 (2013): 478–80, https://pmc.ncbi.nlm.nih.gov/articles/PMC3827523/#:~:text=Hematohidrosis%20is%20a%20very%20rare,%2C%20psychogenic%2C%20and%20unknown%20causes.
22. Isaiah 50:7
23. Hebrews 12:2–3

Learning from Christ's Example

Anxiety doesn't have to be a death sentence to our righteousness, nor our calling in ministry. Not only can we do it scared as we bear with our anxiety day by day, but we can learn from anxiety. In our anxious moments, we can learn how we can display more Christlikeness because of this affliction. Anxiety can go from being a prideful bully to a humble servant teaching us sacred lessons. Certainly, our God can remove the bullies, just like He could've denied Satan's request for Job, answered Paul's prayer to remove his thorn, or somehow allowed Jesus to save mankind while avoiding the agony of crucifixion and God's wrath. If our God chooses to allow our anxieties to remain in some way, it must mean that there is room to learn. His grace will thrust us into Him even more vehemently through every drop of suffering. Turning toward God, during our great storm, ushers us into godliness as we embrace our union with Christ and His promise that we would suffer with Him. Anxiety is not an obstacle in the way of our path; it *is* our path. If all we are trying to do is get over or around our anxiety rather than cling to God as we paddle through our anxiety, we miss the point.

Anxiety doesn't intimidate me like he once did when he held me hostage to his demands. However, there are still times when his presence hits me like a thunderbolt. When that happens, I'm initially caught by surprise, but then I try to figure out why. Why am I surprised when my Savior said we will coexist with both peace and suffering? "I have told you these things so that in me you may have peace. You will have suffering in this world. Be courageous! I have conquered the world."[24] Why am I surprised that agony shows up in the same places as deep faith? Our Savior experienced agony when He was in the garden; His capacity was limited and yet He pushed through its terrors with the strength God gave Him. When He was on the cross, He was even more limited in His ability but He fulfilled God's purpose and will. He did it in order to conquer the world for us. He did it to serve us. He did it thinking not of Himself but of the church. As we keep

24. John 16:33

our eyes on Him rather than having tunnel vision on our suffering, we will find the help and hope to be courageous like our Lord.

I then must make up my mind that unless the Lord appoints a season in my life where I'm bedridden and unable to function, I can do what God has called me to, even if I must "do it scared." I may be trembling, but I will not stop so long as my God has given me breath. I can "do it scared," because my Savior did.

He Must Win the Battle

We've learned our Savior experienced temptation and prevailed as a way to not only save us, but sympathize with us in our spiritual battle. We can put on Christ and stand in Him to resist the serpent seeking to master our lives. We don't have to choose between experiencing the sometimes agonizing pains of anxiety and walking in the will of God. If we are called to both—faith despite our fear—we will not neglect our faith in this life. To whatever God has us walking toward in this season, we can be honest in how we walk toward it: "in weakness with great fear and trembling."[25] We've learned we can walk forward, because our Savior did, despite the stress He endured. We've learned that we can do it, and oftentimes, that means we'll have to do it scared. Like Douglass, we can experience true freedom, even if physically we are restrained. "The snake" can only work in the jurisdiction that our God temporarily allows. Just like the master over Douglass, the grip the enemy has upon us will not penetrate because we know the liberty we have in Christ.

But, when it comes to walking out God's will and calling, there's a day coming when we won't have to "do it scared." We will just do it. No natural or sinful fears attached, and no enemy seeking to tempt and bind. There's a day coming when all we will know is walking forward in the glory, awe, and light of the Lord. There is a place on its way, a home where we won't have to be on guard against constant threats of the enemy, for he will be overthrown for good. Where we

25. 1 Corinthians 2:3

won't have to practice trusting because our faith will no longer be needed, and fear will no longer be a threat. Where the peace of God will be the way of the world. All of which, if we turn the page, leads us to the conclusion of this book.

CONCLUSION

Why the Rain Is Necessary

Not long ago, I woke up every single day feeling anxious. I mean every. single. day. If you're there right now, you know what it's like. You feel the lump in your throat and the *Lub-dub* in your chest. I wish I could sit right there with you. I hurt for you and grieve with you because I know the feeling all too intimately. It feels lonely, and scary, like it will last forever. I pray by now you know it won't.

As you wade through the waves and storms of anxiety, I hope the lessons I learned along my own journey have helped you see that the anxiety which brings you closer to God will always outweigh a considerably calm life that keeps you an arm's distance from Him. I hope the supports I recommended prove fruitful. That with the use of each tool, they are slowly used to help you see that you can climb into the boat and realize Jesus was never asleep. He is right there in the boat with you. When you feel like you have capsized, He is deep in the waters with you. He has been guiding your way all along. The moments He seemed asleep were only to mature your faith in Him and help you better recognize His voice during the trial. You still must deal with the waves as they roar and roll, but now you know you are never alone. Nothing will separate you from the Father's love, not even anxiety. I don't ever want you to forget who is with you and who it is that will never remove His grip. You will not be shipwrecked because of who is with you in it. Whatever your greatest fear, care, or buried emotion, consider that God is with you in it.

I know there's a potential for that last sentence to come off as trite. But I hope you know me a bit better now. I hope you see the primary person I am clinging to and pointing you to—He is truly our hope in this life, whether we wrestle with anxiety or some other struggle. And here's why I say that. In your journey through anxiety, the companions at your side make all the difference. There are a host of options when it comes to companions. And if you had a choice of companion, would you rather choose one who has nice things to say—or the one who overcomes the world? Our ultimate friend in our fear and angst is Christ. He is the only one who will one day undo any and every threat in this life that makes you anxious. And until that day, He will stick with you, even if other companions lose interest, the medicine fails, or the techniques run out. Jesus is the cornerstone, and He is also the pillars holding everything up, including your mind, body, and spirit. Anxiety will not take Him away from you. And so, let anxiety cause you to draw much closer to Him. Right where you are. Let Him guide you through the waters, even as you stand underneath a dark storm cloud releasing a torrential deluge. Let Him bear the weight of that downpour. You may feel like you will always be sullied and saturated by its messiness and catastrophe. In the worst parts of the journey, let Him remind you: He understands, He's been through an even worse downpour, if you can believe it, and it will not always be this way. We can trust His promise of that.

One of my favorite hymns is by Martin Luther titled: "A Mighty Fortress Is Our God."[1] Consider these stanzas (which you can also find in Appendix 1 for quick reference):

> A mighty Fortress is our God,
> A Bulwark never failing;
> Our Helper He amid the flood
> Of mortal ills prevailing:
> For still our ancient foe
> Doth seek to work us woe;
> His craft and power are great,
> And, armed with cruel hate,
> On earth is not his equal.

1. Music and words by Martin Luther (1529). Translated by Frederick Hedge (1853). Public Domain.

Did we in our own strength confide,
Our striving would be losing;
Were not the right Man on our side,
The Man of God's own choosing:
Dost ask who that may be?
Christ Jesus, it is He;
Lord Sabaoth His Name,
From age to age the same,
And He must win the battle.

And though this world, with devils filled,
Should threaten to undo us,
We will not fear, for God hath willed
His truth to triumph through us:
The Prince of Darkness grim,
We tremble not for him;
His rage we can endure,
For lo! his doom is sure,
One little word shall fell him.

We'd all be doomed in our anxiety—or any mortal ill that seems to prevail—"were not the right Man on our side." If left to confide in our own strength, what a terrible condition we would be in. What first-responder or parent looks at a terrified four-year-old, trembling in the wind, screaming for help in the middle of torrential downpour, paddling through its rising flood, and says, "You got this"? God sees us and sends us a "helper amid the flood." Who is it? "Christ Jesus, it is He." And instead of leaving us to somehow fix our fragmented world and frayed nerves on our own, He tells us we don't have to win that battle. "*He* must win the battle." Because we are united to Christ we *will* win the battle, because our Savior fights for us.

God overthrows Satan—along with sin and death. This ancient enemy of humanity, this Prince of Darkness, "we can endure" his rage, as the hymn says, because in the end, "his doom is sure." The Word of God, Christ Himself, "shall fell him." The Bible tells us this will all come to pass, and when it does, it is a glorious picture in Revelation 21, especially if we pay attention to the water elements of the passage:

> Then I saw a new heaven and a new earth; for the first heaven and the first earth had passed away, and ***the sea was no more.*** I also saw the holy city, the new Jerusalem, coming down out of heaven from God, prepared like a bride adorned for her husband. Then I heard a loud voice from the throne: Look, God's dwelling is with humanity, and he will live with them. They will be his peoples, and God himself will be with them and will be their God. He will wipe away every tear from their eyes. Death will be no more; grief, crying, and pain will be no more, because the previous things have passed away. Then the one seated on the throne said, "Look, I am making everything new." He also said, "Write, because these words are faithful and true." Then he said to me, "It is done! I am the Alpha and the Omega, the beginning and the end. I will freely give to the thirsty from the ***spring of the water of life.*** The one who conquers will inherit these things, and I will be his God, and he will be my son.[2]

Throughout this book, I've illustrated my anxious moments using water images (waves, deluges, storms, and so forth), and I've done that on purpose. Why water? Because being clobbered by big strong waves and heavy raindrops is what it actually feels like when you're in the middle of an anxiety attack. Also, water is the basis for life and the living. Water reflects. It shows us ourselves. Water is never static but represents movement, progression, and resonates with our experience as humans. Water represents the power of nature and external forces, pointing to an even more powerful God who created it. And lastly,

---

2. Revelation 21:1–7, emphasis added

Revelation 21 speaks to that image directly when it paints us a picture of our future in a new world.

When God defeats Satan, sin, and death for good, so many wonderful things will be ushered into the new heavens and new earth. But notice what is missing in that blessed reality. The sea. Do you see it? "The sea will be no more." If you remember from chapter 11, we learned that in the Hebrew mind, water was associated with chaos and death—especially the sea. The sea is what would make someone in Bible times tremble. In those days, there was nothing more anxiety-inducing than the sea. It was unpredictable. It was vicious. It would take you down with no mercy.

In the believer's future, we will not have to deal with anything like that ever again, including anxiety. The waves will be gone. The storms will cease. The flood will dry up. Every reason for our anxious trembling—sin, death, and Satan—will be gone. And the sea isn't the only type of water that will be gone. Our tears will be too. Just as God wipes away sin, death, and Satan, He will wipe away the tears they produced. He will wipe away the anxiety that came with them. Why? Because "Death will be no more; grief, crying, and pain will be no more, because the previous things have passed away." The evil one will no longer tempt us or cause us to suffer, for he'll be in the lake of fire himself, learning what it means to suffer judgment. The bodily triggers that throw us into panic will be gone, for our bodies will be resurrected and glorified. The thorns that cause us to shake in weakness as we pursue the will of God will forever be untangled from our existence. Instead of storms and floods, the only form of water we'll experience is "the spring of the water of life"—a reference to the throne of the Father and Son which flows through the Spirit with nothing but grace, mercy, and peace forevermore. On that day, we will tremble. But as the old hymn says of Satan, "we tremble not for him." We will tremble instead, always and only for the Lord. Yes, we will tremble, but only in one blessed way: in awe of our God who makes everything new.

And so, do you want to know why having Christ as your companion through the journey of anxiety is not a trite consolation? Because He's the one who holds the power to make this picture come true. As important as they are in this life, no other tool, support, or helper can promise you this. We may experience many good and important types of ministry from friends, doctors, churches, and medicines as we face anxiety in this life, but none of these can promise to eradicate anxiety entirely—or more than that, usher in a new world where anxiety could not possibly slither in even if it tried. Until that day we walk with Him through the valley, we sing, and we look forward to the day when He will win the battle. Since His kingdom is forever.

In between that glorious day and this dim day, let me leave you with a final thought.

The season of anxiety you are in may seem unfruitful and scarce, but here's the truth: Every care that has led us here to this state of terror—they are not displaced events to cause us to aimlessly jolt and quiver. Rather, they are providential graces to make our trembling an ordained offertory. Again, anxiety's days are numbered. Eventually, our trembling will only be aimed at One. Until then, know that trembling seeds must be placed in the dark soil and die before the flowers bloom. There is a purpose in the water. Each unexpected jolt and drop that pushes us deeper into the shadows of anxieties muddy soil is a gardening tool. A grace used for pruning lilies, myrtle, and roses that come from tiny mustard seeds of faith. God is finishing what He started, therefore—and despite every *Lub-Dub*—we can confidently say it is well with our soul. The holy fragrant bouquet God is composing is proof that every heavy raindrop that makes us tremble is necessary.

Anxious storms rage and mingle with tears.

Water—colors my faith and cares.

Being kept in a raft, God steers.

Tempest Divine, and harvest appears.

APPENDIX 1

Promises, Prayers, Psalms,[1] and Poems

Promises for Your Meditation

Romans 8:38–39

For I am persuaded that neither death nor life, nor angels nor rulers, nor things present nor things to come, nor powers, nor height nor depth, nor any other created thing will be able to separate us from the love of God that is in Christ Jesus our Lord.

Proverbs 12:25

Anxiety in a person's heart weighs it down,
but a good word cheers it up.

Psalm 34:17

The righteous cry out, and the LORD hears,
and rescues them from all their troubles.

1. A sacred song or hymn.

Psalm 55:22

> Cast your burden on the Lord,
> and he will sustain you;
> he will never allow the righteous to be shaken.

Matthew 6:25–34

> "Therefore I tell you: Don't worry about your life, what you will eat or what you will drink; or about your body, what you will wear. Isn't life more than food and the body more than clothing? Consider the birds of the sky: They don't sow or reap or gather into barns, yet your heavenly Father feeds them. Aren't you worth more than they? Can any of you add one moment to his life span by worrying? And why do you worry about clothes? Observe how the wildflowers of the field grow: They don't labor or spin thread. Yet I tell you that not even Solomon in all his splendor was adorned like one of these. If that's how God clothes the grass of the field, which is here today and thrown into the furnace tomorrow, won't he do much more for you—you of little faith? So don't worry, saying, 'What will we eat?' or 'What will we drink?' or 'What will we wear?' For the Gentiles eagerly seek all these things, and your heavenly Father knows that you need them. But seek first the kingdom of God and his righteousness, and all these things will be provided for you. Therefore don't worry about tomorrow, because tomorrow will worry about itself. Each day has enough trouble of its own."

John 16:33

"I have told you these things so that in me you may have peace. You will have suffering in this world. Be courageous! I have conquered the world."

Hebrews 4:12–16

For the word of God is living and effective and sharper than any double-edged sword, penetrating as far as the separation of soul and spirit, joints and marrow. It is able to judge the thoughts and intentions of the heart. No creature is hidden from him, but all things are naked and exposed to the eyes of him to whom we must give an account.

Therefore, since we have a great high priest who has passed through the heavens—Jesus the Son of God—let us hold fast to our confession. For we do not have a high priest who is unable to sympathize with our weaknesses, but one who has been tempted in every way as we are, yet without sin. Therefore, let us approach the throne of grace with boldness, so that we may receive mercy and find grace to help us in time of need.

Isaiah 41:10

"Do not fear, for I am with you;
do not be afraid, for I am your God.
I will strengthen you; I will help you;
I will hold on to you with my righteous right hand."

1 Peter 3:8–17

Finally, all of you be like-minded and sympathetic, love one another, and be compassionate and humble, not paying back evil for evil or insult for insult but, on the contrary, giving a blessing, since you were called for this, so that you may inherit a blessing.

For **the one who wants to love life**
and to see good days,
let him keep his tongue from evil
and his lips from speaking deceit,
and let him turn away from evil
and do what is good.
Let him seek peace and pursue it,
because the eyes of the Lord are on the righteous
and his ears are open to their prayer.
But the face of the Lord is against
those who do what is evil.

Who then will harm you if you are devoted to what is good? But even if you should suffer for righteousness, you are blessed. **Do not fear them or be intimidated**, but in your hearts regard Christ the Lord as holy, ready at any time to give a defense to anyone who asks you for a reason for the hope that is in you. Yet do this with gentleness and reverence, keeping a clear conscience, so that when you are accused, those who disparage your good conduct in Christ will be put to shame. For it is better to suffer for doing good, if that should be God's will, than for doing evil.

Psalm 23

The Lord is my shepherd;
I have what I need.
He lets me lie down in green pastures;
he leads me beside quiet waters.
He renews my life;
he leads me along the right paths
for his name's sake.
Even when I go through the darkest valley,
I fear no danger,
for you are with me;
your rod and your staff—they comfort me.

You prepare a table before me
in the presence of my enemies;
you anoint my head with oil;
my cup overflows.
Only goodness and faithful love will pursue me
all the days of my life,
and I will dwell in the house of the Lord
as long as I live.

Luke 10:40–42

But Martha was distracted by her many tasks, and she came up and asked, "Lord, don't you care that my sister has left me to serve alone? So tell her to give me a hand."

The Lord answered her, "Martha, Martha, you are worried and upset about many things, but one thing is necessary. Mary has made the right choice, and it will not be taken away from her."

Philippians 4:6–9

Don't worry about anything, but in everything, through prayer and petition with thanksgiving, present your requests to God. And the peace of God, which surpasses all understanding, will guard your hearts and minds in Christ Jesus.

Finally brothers and sisters, whatever is true, whatever is honorable, whatever is just, whatever is pure, whatever is lovely, whatever is commendable—if there is any moral excellence and if there is anything praiseworthy—dwell on these things. Do what you have learned and received and heard from me, and seen in me, and the God of peace will be with you.

2 Thessalonians 3:16

May the Lord of peace himself give you peace always in every way. The Lord be with all of you.

Psalm 56:3

When I am afraid,
I will trust in you.

Prayers to Aid Your Abdication

A prayer when dealing with natural fear

God of love,

There is no fear of judgment because the sacrificial love of my Savior has blotted guilt from my record. Through Your mercy You have delivered me from my sin and yet through Your divine wisdom You have allowed sanctification through the means of this fallen body, that I may learn to suffer with Christ. As my body trembles, uphold me in Your care. Comfort me in Your peace. Fill me with Your Spirit. Make much of Yourself in my powerlessness. May thankfulness and praise be my disposition all of my days.

Only with Your help and strength,
And in the name of my Savior who also trembled,
Amen.

A prayer when dealing with sinful fear

God of Righteousness,

You are holy, holy, holy. My inability to meet Your standard shows me that I am not.

As I sit in my fears, overwhelmed by my sin, please forgive me for placing people, things, and my thoughts above You. Break me free from my idols. Help me repent and prioritize You and Your words first in my life. May You be my treasure that I give all else up for.

Thank You for Your pardon because of Jesus Christ the righteous who died on the cross for sinners and was resurrected from the grave to show He is sufficiently resourced to save and sanctify.

In Jesus's name,
Amen.

A prayer of reverential fear

God Almighty,

Your ways are far above ours. Your power extends beyond our understanding. Because of Your perfect presence, we tremble. We fall down and bow before You, in humility. We declare that You alone are God. You are the perfection of beauty and majesty. May You increase and we further decrease.

Help us to revere You rightly, oh Most High God. Help us to live in light of Your omnipotence. For You are God. We are not God. May Your holiness be known throughout the earth, including in our hearts. Help us to praise You for Your glorious strength in private and public—teach us to magnify You. Let us never be afraid to tremble for You, the God who declares, "I AM WHO I AM" (Exod. 3:14).

In Jesus's holy name,

Amen.

Prayers to Counteract "What-If" and "If-Then" Statements

God, I'm hyperfocused upon what other people might be thinking about me and it's making me feel incompetent. Would You help me to root myself in what Your Word says about me and not be given to the fear of man?

Father, I'm a people pleaser because I think saying "no" will let those around me down. Lord, help me to trust You and have boundaries that prioritize You rather than those I seek to please.

God, I am worried about my marriage, and it has my mind spiraling. Help me remember I am not in control of my spouse. My ruminating thoughts will not heal my marriage. Please, remind me that no matter what,

You are with me and I am safe in You. God, would You minister to us both, so that we would honor You and each other?

Lord, I am concerned that I might die. I feel so much fear. God, would You remind me of what Your Word says about death? Please comfort me when my mind catastrophes and remind me of my imperishable hope.

God, I am tempted to doubt whether or not You have redeemed me. Would You remind me of Your work in my life, despite how I feel today? Flood my mind with truths from Your Word that declare my redemption and acceptance through the work of Your Son. Help me reach out to fellow Christians, asking for their help in moments it's hard to remember the truth of my redemption.

In Jesus's name,
Amen.

Psalms to Prompt Adoration

"A Mighty Fortress Is Our God" by Martin Luther

A mighty Fortress is our God,
A Bulwark never failing;
Our Helper He amid the flood
Of mortal ills prevailing:
For still our ancient foe
Doth seek to work us woe;
His craft and power are great,
And, armed with cruel hate,
On earth is not his equal.

Did we in our own strength confide,
Our striving would be losing;
Were not the right Man on our side,
The Man of God's own choosing:
Dost ask who that may be?
Christ Jesus, it is He;
Lord Sabaoth His Name,
From age to age the same,
And He must win the battle.

And though this world, with devils filled,
Should threaten to undo us,
We will not fear, for God hath willed
His truth to triumph through us:
The Prince of Darkness grim,
We tremble not for him;
His rage we can endure,
For lo! his doom is sure,
One little word shall fell him.

That word above all earthly powers,
No thanks to them, abideth;
The Spirit and the gifts are ours
Through Him who with us sideth:
Let goods and kindred go,
This mortal life also;
The body they may kill:
God's truth abideth still,
His Kingdom is forever.

"Prayer Answered by Crosses" by John Newton

I asked the Lord that I might grow
In faith, and love, and every grace;
Might more of His salvation know,
And seek, more earnestly, His face.

'Twas He who taught me thus to pray,
And He, I trust, has answered prayer!
But it has been in such a way,
As almost drove me to despair.

I hoped that in some favored hour,
At once He'd answer my request;
And by His love's constraining pow'r,
Subdue my sins, and give me rest.

Instead of this, He made me feel
The hidden evils of my heart;
And let the angry pow'rs of hell
Assault my soul in every part.

Yea more, with His own hand He seemed
Intent to aggravate my woe;
Crossed all the fair designs I schemed,
Blasted my gourds, and laid me low.

Lord, why is this, I trembling cried,
Wilt thou pursue thy worm to death?
"'Tis in this way," the Lord replied,
"I answer prayer for grace and faith."

"These inward trials I employ,
From self, and pride, to set thee free;
And break thy schemes of earthly joy,
That thou may'st find thy all in Me."

"Be Still My Soul" by Katharina von Schlegel (1752), Translator: Jane Borthwick (1855)

Be still, my soul: the Lord is on thy side
Bear patiently the cross of grief or pain.
Leave to thy God to order and provide;
In every change, He faithful will remain,

Be still, my soul: thy best, thy heavenly Friend
Through thorny ways leads to a joyful end.

Be still, my soul: thy God doth undertake
To guide the future, as He has the past.
Thy hope, thy confidence let nothing shake;
All now mysterious shall be bright at last.

Be still, my soul: the waves and winds still know
His voice Who ruled them while He dwelt below.

"Under His Care" by Frances R. Havergal

God will take care of you all thro' the day;
He who has loved you so keeps you from ill;
Waking or resting, at work or at play,
He will be with you and watching you still.

God will take care of you all thro' the night,
Holding thy hand, He so tenderly keeps;
Darkness to Him is the same as the light;
He never slumbers and He never sleeps.

God will take care of you all thro' the year,
Crowning each day with His kindness and love,
Sending you blessings and shielding from fear,
Leading you on to that bright home above.

Chorus

Under His care;
Under His care;
Safely I'm dwelling while under His care.

Our Resurrected Hope Amid Suffering by Blair Linne

Suffering never tastes sweet

Never mango ripe

It is a bitter cup

A thorn in our flesh

A hip out of joint

Suffering is imitating God.

Reminds us of our Savior, don't it?

Our God who never broke a bone, but was broken bare

Raw like an open wound,

He remained.

When the sky turned the shade of coffee grains

As black and bitter as His pain.

Although He is the Truth, He refused to open His mouth when He raised His hands.

Surrendered to the paradox.

Looked death square in the eye, because He knew His Father had the wheel.

—Was the pilot when He was handed over to Pilate.

Exchanged for Barabbas. No guilt but received sins wages,

what humility.

—To bleed for only ever doing good.

To bear the yoke of God's fatal fury for a foe.

Forgive a finite fool and call him friend, forever.

For, no evil ever rested on the tip of His tongue Yet, He never tiptoed around the pain.

When they held Him with nails ordained.

He never rolled His eyes or sucked His teeth

He chose death to live free in the will of God.

Our Savior knows suffering.

Mastered it.

From the pain of putting on flesh To the agony of literally loving someone to death.

He wrestled hell's horrors and won.

Strangled the prowling lion, whose kisses do more harm than Judas's kisses ever could

You see He conquered for us. Amputated the arms of the grave

Rolled the stone back, back, back and away, Like how our sins rolled away

when He rose again that day.

A servant is not greater than his or her Master.

We are united with the Suffering Servant. So why do we think we should be exempt?

That our Christlikeness only applies when things seem easy.

When we only want the gifts that we deem a blessing

We forget that suffering is often the package they arrive in.

Suffering is a fist full of shrapnel aimed at our head and heart.

Cuts away the flesh, the vainglory, the self-sufficiency

Turns our "me" to mercy, our "I" to insignificant.

It is a heavy load, but we shrink in the wash.

Leaves us low, and grateful, and Christlike, and ready for glory

Makes us tremble and long for our Lord's return.

Suffering is a tool in the hand of our God to make us holy, and always relying.

It is a thousand useful graces which help solidify our hope.

So when the world whispers sorrow in our ear,

And we are tempted to make self-pity our home, May we run to our only Shelter.

When the devil calls us by our first name Do not rebuke him but recall his fate.

Leave him in the hands of our God Who can strike a blow with one breath.

Who will return and take us home within the twinkling of an eye. In a flash.

Suffering will be over when our Resurrection cracks the sky.

When anxiety causes us to shatter like folded stained glass Remember

the color Remember

the beauty in brokenness Remember

we are a sanctuary, A frail cathedral.

The greater the awareness of weakness, the more we depend,

by His grace. Remember

how with more shards come more opportunities for light to travel. Remember

your God Remember

your living hope Remember . . .

When your body, and mind feel brittle like bark ready to break,

Anxiety is smothering you with her lies Tempting you to fear the truth. Remember

God's words. Remember

to meditate when inclined to forget. Remember

we are to be a tree: We live in the harsh sun and tumultuous water,

It helps us bear fruit in season. Our leaves are alive God is holding our body together.

Although outwardly perishing, inwardly we are being renewed.

Broken, yet blessed.

Hope is discovered in the night of adversity

We are living stones, collectively built upon that glorious Rock and His glorious words.

—Neither of which will ever perish. So may no evil ever rest on the tip of our tongue

May we never tiptoe around the pain, when we are held, with nails ordained.

May we never roll our eyes or suck our teeth but choose death r to live free

in the will of God.

May we bear up under these trials with joy.

Always remembering our God

Remembering our Living Hope

Remembering our Resurrection

Remembering we were **Made to Tremble.**

And everything God made is good.

APPENDIX 2

Breathing Technique

During one of my counseling sessions, I was taught how breathing can help with calming since it affects our nervous system, reduces heart rate and blood pressure, and gets more oxygen circulating within our body. I have often used this technique to help me. The reason why deep breathing is helpful is because when we are anxious, our breathing is shallow, and the reduced oxygen intake makes us feel more anxious because it signals to our body that we are in a state of alert. Controlling your breathing is a practical way to help regulate some of your symptoms.

Instructions

Place one hand on your chest, and the other on your belly, holding your diaphragm. Try a full abdominal breath. Breathe in slowly and regularly without a big breath. Inhale (1-2-3-4-5) and then slowly exhale (1-2-3-4-5) pausing at the end of each.

- Take a deep breath in through your nose for (1- 2- 3- 4- 5) pause.
- Breathe out of your mouth gently for (1- 2- 3- 4-5) pause.

Try this several times. If you start to feel light-headed, stop for a few minutes and then you can try again.

Breathe in . . . **"God is in control, and I am safe in Him."** Breathe out (1-2-3-4-5) . . .

Or, **"cool air in (1-2-3-4-5), warm air out (1-2-3-4-5), I am safe in Christ."**

We can breathe. Trust. Rest secure. God rules over our nervous system. He helps us breathe.

We are not God. We are safe in God.

APPENDIX 3

Resources for Individuals with Anxiety and Their Pastors and Ministry Leaders

In a book like this, it would be doing you a disservice not to include information on what to do if you need help.

1. For the suicide and crisis lifeline, call or text 988: an easy-to-remember, three-digit code that connects people to a suicide crisis counselor 24/7. (This was formerly known as the National Suicide Prevention Lifeline.) You can also go to https://988lifeline.org/. You do not have to be suicidal or even have any suicidal thoughts to call this number. Counselors are there to help you through any crisis and connect you, if you're interested, to local services.
2. Another helpful online resource is the Anxiety and Depression Association of America website: https://adaa.org/understanding-anxiety.
3. If you're looking for a counselor, I recommend CCEF: biblical counseling counselors, resources, and courses (see https://www.ccef.org/about).
4. If you are looking for a therapist, Diane Langberg offers counseling to trauma survivors, families, and clergy (see https://langbergmonroe.com).

5. Lastly, perhaps Grief Share is right for you if you're looking to find a grief support group in your area (see https://www.griefshare.org).

How to Choose a Therapist

1. Consider your health insurance; your plan may have a provider network or may reimburse out-of-network providers; find out if there is a copay, limited number of sessions, sliding scale, etc.
2. Ask for a discounted or free first meeting or call to discuss their services and your needs and potential fit.
3. Search therapist databases online. You can find these by searching "find a therapist near me."
4. Think about your goals ahead of time.

    Goal considerations: medication, cognitive focus, emotional focus, relational focus, skills focus, trauma focus, individual/couple/group

5. Be open to evidence-based interventions, even if you're not familiar with them.
6. Do your research and ask questions.

Some Questions You Might Ask Potential Therapists[1]

1. Are you a licensed psychologist/counselor in this state?
2. How many years have you been in practice?

1. The advice represented below is from Bobbi Jo Yarborough, a member of my church who is also a clinical psychologist and mental health service researcher. She recently gave a talk on anxiety, and these bullet points are her advice on choosing a therapist and some questions to ask.

3. What do you consider to be your area of expertise/specialty? (Beware, some people list more specialties than they can possibly be experts in!)
4. What experience do you have treating someone with my issue? How do you usually treat someone with my issue?
5. How long do you expect treatment to last? How soon could I expect to start feeling better?
6. Do you accept my insurance? Will I need to pay you and be reimbursed or will you bill directly?
7. What are your fees?
8. If I need medication, can you prescribe it or recommend someone who does? How will you coordinate my care with that person?
9. Do you do telehealth/virtual visits? Do you do in-person visits? How often might I expect to see you?
10. What will we do if the treatment plan isn't working?
11. Pay attention to your own responses to the psychologist/therapist.
12. You should feel comfortable, heard, respected.
13. They should start/end on time, be curious, listen carefully (not interrupt), guide you.
14. Do you incorporate prayer and the Holy Scriptures in your practice? If not, how do you think about respecting the religious beliefs of your clients? *Ethically, it is a requirement of licensed professionals to suspend their own beliefs and biases unless they are invited by the client to share them.*

Questions for Pastors/Friends to Consider as They Seek to Help Anxious Loved Ones

Here are some questions to keep in mind:

- What should you do if you or someone you know has a mental health crisis? Do you have a plan?
- Who will advocate for the single people in your congregation struggling with anxiety?
- How do we foster community so that real relationships are established beyond Sunday mornings?
- Could we create a benevolence fund in the case of counseling needs?
- Are there any trained counselors who could come in and host a session, training all the church leaders on the basics of how to recognize and refer for mental health care?
- Is there space for men to be vulnerable with their stressful concerns in your congregation?
- What is our plan of action if someone in our congregation is suicidal?
- How can my sermon application speak to those who are anxious, depressed, or overwhelmed this week?
- Does our church library have helpful resources for families walking through a mental health crisis?
- How can I exalt God's comforting power when I counsel those around me who are anxious?
- Do we preach shame or security in God when mental health comes up?
- Do the leaders of the church have a healthy work-life balance or are they on the verge of burnout from stress?

- When sabbaticals are taken, is it to invest in families and rest, or to write books and prioritize more work?

A Word to Church Leaders

Ministry leaders, you've likely already run into people in your ministry who struggle with anxiety. It is imperative for us to be trained well. This doesn't mean that you become a professional counselor; rather, it means it's wise to be aware of the anxiety crisis in our culture right now, and to teach, lead, and disciple around this issue. Here are some ideas for ministry leaders to do this well:

Don't use blanket statements or simplistic, reductionistic teachings about fear or anxiety. For example, the teaching that "all fear is sin," or that "the opposite of fear is faith," or that "F.E.A.R. means False Events Appearing as Real." I first heard these teachings at church when I was a teen. Spoken without any nuance or explanation regarding healthy fears versus unhealthy fears, I thought every single fear I had was sinful. That's just not true; especially if one of your congregants just faced a situation when they had to run away from very real danger or woke up in the night with PTSD symptoms. Fear is not always the result of sin. When fear or anxiety is a bodily response in a believer due to trauma or something else, faith is still right there with us. We are kept by God, despite our bodily response of living in a fallen world. Fear being the opposite of faith is a false dichotomy. It causes many of us to question our standing before God despite God never stating that our fear disqualifies us from His unconditional love. If that were the case, then Paul must've not really been a Christian, for he mentions being anxious more than once![2]

Scripture teaches that the opposite of faith is not fear, but unbelief. We are not condemned for having fear or anxiety. We are condemned if we do not have a relationship with God. Being in that place of unbelief brings with it a type of fear, that is a terror because we are under

2. Philippians 2:28; 2 Corinthians 11:28

God's judgment. We are condemned only when we do not know the love of the Lord.[3] For those of us who belong to God, we do not have to worry about judgment from God, nor do we have to worry about being cast out because of our anxiety. God's *chesed*, or steadfast lovingkindness, along with His perfect love, removes fear based on punishment.[4] When Christians experience angst, we are not cursed forevermore, we are met with grace and help in our time of need,[5] and we are reminded of God's tender presence as He walks with us in our anxiety. When we fear the future, God reminds us of our eternal future with Him and calms our fears with His consolations.[6] Yes, it is true that His instructions "do not fear" throughout Scripture are commands, but God helps us obey those commands by *reminding* us of our gospel identity, not threatening its very existence.

Know your capacity limits (and the culture of your leadership environment). Many pastors (and many times, women's ministry leaders too!) can't minister to the anxiety in other people because they themselves are anxiety-ridden. There are many reasons for this, but one of them is that leaders like this don't know how to rest. Sabbaticals are taken but not used to rest and be revived; they are for writing books, hosting conferences, and/or debating on social media. That anxious toil trickles down to the congregants. We think we always must have something going. Doing all the things. Never resting at God's feet like Mary. We keep grinding. Feeling like we need to do more. We are little anxious bunnies, going and going and going, until we can't. The anxious toil makes us feel worthy and valued and good. It makes us forget that we are mortal for just a little bit. I rarely hear anyone talking about living a peaceful and quiet life anymore[7] because we are so used to living in a world that rewards toil and anxious striving. If the people in the pews are anxious, perhaps consider if that's because it's coming from the culture of the leadership.

3. 1 Corinthians 16:22
4. 1 John 4:18
5. Hebrews 4:16
6. Psalm 94:19
7. 1 Timothy 2:2; 1 Thessalonians 4:11

Know your expertise limits. If someone in your congregation is struggling with a mental health concern, that doesn't mean they merely need discipleship. They do need discipleship, but they may also need a therapist. They should not be forced to choose one or the other. A dear friend of mine I met with shared some self-harm tendencies and I encouraged her to consider getting a counselor. Her pastor heard about it and said, "You don't need a counselor, I will meet with you." He was untrained, and it did not help her much at all. Years later she has gotten counseling and is on the road to recovery. Being a pastor doesn't mean being an expert at every issue in the mind and body. Since not all issues stem from a spiritual lack, bearing the burdens of those under your watch can mean either hiring out a counselor/psychiatrist or working alongside this expert to make sure your congregant is resourced in a robust way.

Related to that, just as you wouldn't fix a person with a gunshot wound by reading Scripture, we shouldn't expect all our mental ills to vanish through reading Scripture alone. While the God of the Bible can certainly heal our mental afflictions, the Bible is not a mental health workbook. While we do find great wisdom in the Bible, it also encourages us to seek counsel and wisdom from others. It is okay to stop the bleeding first, bandage up the body, and then encourage them with Scripture. With our mind, I would say, use the Word to bring encouragement and comfort, and encourage professional medical treatment and/or licensed counselors who may use a variety of helpful techniques depending upon the issue. The Scriptures transform the mind, yes and amen. Don't hear me say it holds no power. At the same time, many other external things help the mind work properly as well—things like hydrating so the brain has enough water to function, therapy so the mind can come out of "fight-or-flight" mode, and medication so that biological and neurological problems are treated adequately. With all these things working together, and all members of the body offering their expertise, your congregant has a much better chance at getting healthier in their mental struggles.